INTRODUCTION TO
Economic Growth

INTRODUCTION TO
ECONOMIC GROWTH

CHARLES I. JONES STANFORD UNIVERSITY

 W. W. NORTON & COMPANY NEW YORK LONDON

First Edition

The text of this book is composed in Melior with
the display set in McKinley.
Composition by Integre Technical Publishing Co., Inc.
Manufacturing by Courier
Book design by Jack Meserole

Library of Congress Cataloging-in-Publication Data
Jones, Charles I. (Charles Irving)
    Introduction to economic growth / Charles I. Jones.
        p.   cm.
    Includes bibliographical references and index.
    ISBN 0-393-97174-0
    1. Economic development.   2. Economic indicators.   I. Title.
HD75.J66   1997
338.9—dc21   97-8349

W. W. Norton & Company, Inc., 500 Fifth Avenue, New York, N.Y. 10110
    http://www.wwnorton.com

W. W. Norton & Company Ltd., 10 Coptic Street, London WC1A 1PU

    4 5 6 7 8 9 0

To my parents

CONTENTS

6 A SIMPLE MODEL OF GROWTH AND DEVELOPMENT   115

7 INFRASTRUCTURE AND LONG-RUN ECONOMIC PERFORMANCE   127

8 ALTERNATIVE THEORIES OF ENDOGENOUS GROWTH   147

PREFACE

The importance of economic growth is difficult to overstate. The more than tenfold increase in income in the United States over the last century is the result of economic growth. So is the fact that incomes in the United States and Western Europe are at least thirty times greater than incomes in much of sub-Saharan Africa.

Our understanding of economic growth has improved enormously in the last fifteen years. Since the mid-1980s, growth has been one of the most active fields of research in economics. Yet while the advances in research now play a very prominent role in academic discourse and graduate education, they have not filtered through to the undergraduate level. A large part of the reason for this neglect is that these advances have been discussed primarily in academic journals. The result is a collection of fascinating but highly technical publications replete with mathematics, the modern language of economics.

This book translates these contributions into a more accessible language. The fundamental insights of old and new growth theory are explained with an emphasis on economics instead of math. No mathematics beyond the first-semester calculus taught at most colleges and universities is required. Moreover, the bulk of the required mathematics is introduced with the Solow model in Chapter 2; the analysis in subsequent chapters merely uses the same tools over and over again.[1]

---

[1]Two key simplifications enhance the accessibility of the material covered in this book. First, the models are presented without dynamic optimization. Second, the data analysis is conducted without econometrics.

This book should prove useful in undergraduate courses on economic growth, as well as in courses on macroeconomics, advanced macroeconomics, and economic development. Graduate students may find it valuable as a companion to the more advanced treatments available in the original journal articles and elsewhere. Finally, I hope that my colleagues will discover new insights in a place or two; I have certainly learned a tremendous amount in the process of preparing the manuscript.

I am deeply grateful to Robert Barro, Susanto Basu, Sunny Jones, Michael Kremer, Paul Romer, Xavier Sala-i-Martin, Bobby Sinclair, Terry Tao, John Williams, and Alwyn Young for their encouragement and for comments on earlier drafts. I also owe thanks to the National Science Foundation for a CAREER grant (SBR-9510916) that encouraged me to teach economic growth in my undergraduate courses.

Charles I. Jones
Stanford University
Summer 1997

INTRODUCTION TO

ECONOMIC GROWTH

INTRODUCTION: THE FACTS OF ECONOMIC GROWTH

"The errors which arise from the absence of facts are far more numerous and more durable than those which result from unsound reasoning respecting true data."
> — CHARLES BABBAGE, quoted in Rosenberg (1994), p. 27.

"It is quite wrong to try founding a theory on observable magnitudes alone.... It is the theory which decides what we can observe."
> — ALBERT EINSTEIN, quoted in Heisenberg (1971), p. 63.

Speaking at the annual meeting of the American Economic Association in 1989, the renowned economic historian David S. Landes chose as the title of his address the fundamental question of economic growth and development: "Why Are We So Rich and They So Poor?"[1] This age-old question has preoccupied economists for centuries. The question so fascinated the classical economists that it was stamped on the cover of Adam Smith's famous treatise *An Inquiry into the Nature and Causes of the Wealth of Nations*. And it was the mistaken forecast of Thomas Malthus in the early nineteenth century concerning the future prospects for economic growth that earned the discipline its most recognized epithet, the "dismal science."

---

[1] See Landes (1990).

The modern examination of this question by macroeconomists dates to the 1950s and the publication of two famous papers by Robert Solow of the Massachusetts Institute of Technology. Solow's theories helped to clarify the role of the accumulation of physical capital and emphasized the importance of technological progress as the ultimate driving force behind sustained economic growth. During the 1960s and to a lesser extent the 1970s, work on economic growth flourished.[2] For methodological reasons, however, important aspects of the theoretical exploration of technological change were postponed.[3]

In the early 1980s, work at the University of Chicago by Paul Romer and Robert Lucas re-ignited the interest of macroeconomists in economic growth, emphasizing the economics of "ideas" and of human capital. Taking advantage of new developments in the theory of imperfect competition, Romer introduced the economics of technology to macroeconomists. Following these theoretical advances, empirical work by a number of economists, such as Robert Barro of Harvard University, emerged to quantify and test the theories of growth. Both theoretical and empirical work has continued with enormous professional interest in the 1990s.

The purpose of this book is to explain and explore the modern theories of economic growth. This exploration is an exciting journey, in which we encounter several ideas that have already earned Nobel Prizes and several more with Nobel potential. The book attempts to make this cutting-edge research accessible to readers with only basic training in economics and calculus.[4]

The approach of this book is similar to the approach scientists take in studying astronomy and cosmology. Like economists, astronomers are unable to perform the controlled experiments that are the hallmark of chemistry and physics. Astronomy proceeds instead through an interplay between observation and theory. There is observation: planets,

---

[2] A far from exhaustive list of contributors includes Moses Abramovitz, Kenneth Arrow, David Cass, Tjalling Koopmans, Simon Kuznets, Richard Nelson, William Nordhaus, Edmund Phelps, Karl Shell, Eytan Sheshinski, Trevor Swan, Hirofumi Uzawa, and Carl von Weizsacker.

[3] Romer (1994) provides a nice discussion of this point and of the history of research on economic growth.

[4] The reader with advanced training is referred also to the excellent presentation in Barro and Sala-i-Martin (1995).

stars, and galaxies are laid out across the universe in a particular way. Galaxies are moving apart, and the universe appears to be sparsely populated with occasional "lumps" of matter. And there is theory: the theory of the Big Bang, for example, provides a coherent explanation for these observations.

This same interplay between observation and theory is used to organize this book. This first chapter will outline the broad empirical regularities associated with growth and development. How rich are the rich countries, how poor are the poor? How fast do rich and poor countries grow? The remainder of the book consists of theories to explain these observations. In the limited pages we have before us, we will not spend much time on the experiences of individual countries, although these experiences are very important. Instead, the goal is to provide a general economic framework to help us understand the process of growth and development.

A critical difference between astronomy and economics, of course, is that the economic "universe" can potentially be re-created by economic policy. Unlike the watchmaker who builds a watch and then leaves it to run forever, economic policy makers constantly shape the course of growth and development. A prerequisite to better policies is a better understanding of economic growth.

1.1 THE DATA OF GROWTH AND DEVELOPMENT

The world consists of economies of all shapes and sizes. There are very rich countries, and there are very poor countries. Some economies are growing rapidly, and some are not growing at all. Finally, a large number of economies — most, in fact — lie between these extremes. In thinking about economic growth and development, it is helpful to begin by considering the extreme cases: the rich, the poor, and the countries that are moving rapidly in between. The remainder of this chapter lays out the empirical evidence — the "facts" — associated with these categories. The key questions of growth and development then almost naturally ask themselves.

Table 1.1 displays some basic data on growth and development for seventeen countries. We will focus our discussion of the data on measures of per capita income instead of reporting data such as life

TABLE 1.1 STATISTICS ON GROWTH AND DEVELOPMENT

	GDP per capita, 1990	GDP per worker, 1990	Labor force participation rate, 1990	Average annual growth rate, 1960–90	Years to double
"Rich" countries					
U.S.A.	$18,073	$36,810	0.49	1.4	51
West Germany	14,331	29,488	0.49	2.5	28
Japan	14,317	22,602	0.63	5.0	14
France	13,896	30,340	0.46	2.7	26
U.K.	13,223	26,767	0.49	2.0	35
"Poor" countries					
China	1,324	2,189	0.60	2.4	29
India	1,262	3,230	0.39	2.0	35
Zimbabwe	1,181	2,435	0.49	0.2	281
Uganda	554	1,142	0.49	−0.2	−281
"Growth miracles"					
Hong Kong	14,854	22,835	0.65	5.7	12
Singapore	11,698	24,344	0.48	5.3	13
Taiwan	8,067	18,418	0.44	5.7	12
South Korea	6,665	16,003	0.42	6.0	12
"Growth disasters"					
Venezuela	6,070	17,469	0.35	−0.5	−136
Madagascar	675	1,561	0.43	−1.3	−52
Mali	530	1,105	0.48	−1.0	−70
Chad	400	1,151	0.35	−1.7	−42

SOURCE: Penn World Tables Mark 5.6, an update of Summers and Heston (1991), and author's calculations.

Notes: The GDP data are in 1985 dollars. The growth rate is the average annual change in the log of GDP per worker. A negative number in the "Years to double" column indicates "years to halve."

expectancy, infant mortality, or other measures of quality of life. The main reason for this focus is that the theories we develop in subsequent chapters will be couched in terms of per capita income. Furthermore, per capita income is a useful "summary statistic" of the level of economic development in the sense that it is highly correlated with other measures of quality of life.[5]

We will interpret Table 1.1 in the context of some "facts," beginning with the first:[6]

FACT # 1   **There is enormous variation in per capita income across economies. The poorest countries have per capita incomes that are less than 5 percent of per capita incomes in the richest countries.**

The first section of Table 1.1 reports real per capita gross domestic product (GDP) in 1990, together with some other data, for the United States and several other "rich" countries. The United States was the richest country in the world in 1990, with a per capita GDP of $18,073 (in 1985 dollars), and it was the richest by a substantial amount — countries such as Japan and West Germany trailed around the $14,300 mark.

These numbers may at first seem slightly surprising. One often reads in newspapers that the United States has fallen behind countries like Japan or Germany in terms of per capita income. Such newspaper accounts can be misleading, however, because market exchange rates are typically used in the comparison. U.S. GDP is measured in dollars, while Japanese GDP is measured in yen. How do we convert the Japanese yen to dollars in order to make a comparison? One way is to use prevailing exchange rates. For example, in January 1997, the yen–dollar exchange rate was around 120 yen per dollar. However, exchange rates can be extremely volatile. Just a little over one year earlier, the rate was only 100 yen per dollar. Which of these exchange rates is "right"? Obviously, it matters a great deal which one we use: at 100 yen per dollar, Japan will seem 20 percent richer than at 120 yen per dollar.

---

[5] See, for example, the World Bank's *World Development Report, 1991* (New York: Oxford University Press, 1991).
[6] Many of these facts have been discussed elsewhere. See especially Lucas (1988) and Romer (1989).

Instead of relying on prevailing exchange rates to make international comparisons of GDP, economists attempt to measure the actual value of a currency in terms of its ability to purchase similar products. The resulting conversion factor is sometimes called a purchasing power parity–adjusted exchange rate. For example, the *Economist* magazine produces a yearly report of purchasing power parity (PPP) exchange rates based on the price of a McDonald's Big Mac hamburger. If a Big Mac costs 2 dollars in the United States and 300 yen in Japan, then the PPP exchange rate based on the Big Mac is 150 yen per dollar. By extending this method to a number of different goods, economists construct a PPP exchange rate that can be applied to GDP. Such calculations suggest that 150 yen per dollar is a much better number than the prevailing exchange rates of 100 or 120 yen per dollar.[7]

The second column of Table 1.1 reports a related measure, real GDP per worker in 1990. The difference between the two columns lies in the denominator: the first column divides total GDP by a country's entire population, while the second column divides GDP by only the labor force. The third column reports the 1990 labor force participation rate — the ratio of the labor force to the population — to show the relationship between the first two columns. Notice that while Japan and West Germany had similar per capita GDP in 1990, they had very different GDP per worker. The labor force participation rate is much higher in Japan than in the other industrialized countries.

Which column should we use in comparing levels of development? The answer depends on what question is being asked. Perhaps per capita GDP is a more general measure of welfare in that it tells us how much output per person is available to be consumed, invested, or put to some other use. On the other hand, GDP per worker tells us more about the productivity of the labor force. In this sense, the first statistic can be thought of as a welfare measure, while the second is a productivity measure. This seems to be a reasonable way to interpret these measures, but one can also make the case for using GDP per worker as a welfare measure. Persons not officially counted as being in the labor force may be engaged in "home production" or may work in the underground economy. Neither of these activities is included in GDP, and in this case measured output divided by measured labor input may prove more

---

[7] *Economist*, April 19, 1995, p. 74.

accurate for making welfare comparisons. In this book, we will often use the phrase "per capita income" as a generic welfare measure, even when speaking of GDP per worker, if the context is clear. Whatever measure we use, though, Table 1.1 tells us one of the first key things about economic development: the more "effort" an economy puts into producing output, the more output there is to go around. "Effort" in this context corresponds to the labor force participation rate.

The second section of Table 1.1 documents the relative and even absolute poverty of some of the world's poorest economies. India and Zimbabwe had per capita GDPs around $1,000 in 1990, little more than 5 percent of per capita GDP in the United States. A number of economies in sub-Saharan Africa are even poorer: per capita income in the United States is more than 40 times higher than income in Ethiopia.

To place these numbers in perspective, consider some other statistics. The typical worker in Ethiopia or Uganda must work a month and a half to earn what the typical worker in the United States earns in a day. Life expectancy in Ethiopia is only two-thirds that in the United States, and infant mortality is more than 20 times higher. Approximately 40 percent of GDP is spent on food in Ethiopia, compared to about 7 percent in the United States.

What fraction of the world's population lives with this kind of poverty? Figure 1.1 answers this question by plotting the distribution of the world's population in terms of GDP per worker. In 1988, nearly half of the world's population lived in countries with less than 10 percent of U.S. GDP per worker. The bulk of this population lives in only two countries: China, with more than one-fifth of the world's population, had a GDP per worker of less than one-fifteenth of that of the United States; India, with one-sixth of the world's population, had a GDP per worker less than one-tenth that of the United States. Together, these two countries account for nearly 40 percent of the world's population. In contrast, the 39 countries that make up sub-Saharan Africa constitute less than 10 percent of the world's population.

Figure 1.2 shows how this distribution has changed since 1960. Overall, the distribution has equalized as the share of the world's population living in countries with GDP per worker less than 30 percent of U.S. GDP has fallen, largely shifting into the 40 percent and 50 percent categories. Of the poorest countries, both China and India have seen substantial growth in GDP per worker, even relative to the United

FIGURE 1.1 CUMULATIVE DISTRIBUTION OF WORLD POPULATION BY GDP PER WORKER, 1988

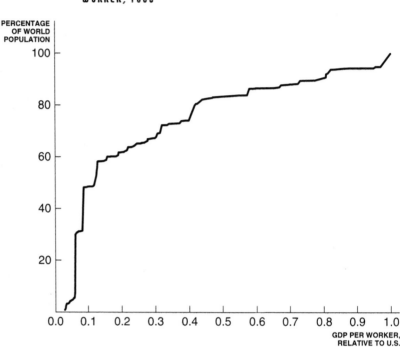

SOURCE: Penn World Tables Mark 5.6, Summers and Heston (1991).

Note: A point (x, y) in the figure indicates that the fraction of the world's population living in countries with a relative GDP per worker less than x is equal to y. 140 countries are included.

States. China's relative income rose from 4 percent of U.S. GDP in 1960 to 6 percent in 1988, and India's relative income rose from 7 percent of U.S. GDP to 9 percent over the same period.

The third section of Table 1.1 reports data for several countries that are moving from the second group to the first. These four so-called newly industrializing countries (NICs) are Hong Kong, Singapore, Taiwan, and South Korea. Interestingly, by 1990 Hong Kong had a per capita GDP of $14,854, higher than all of the industrialized countries in the table except for the United States. This per capita GDP was more than twice that of South Korea. However, as with Japan, Hong Kong's high per capita GDP is driven to a large extent by its high labor force participation rate. In terms of GDP per worker, Hong Kong is roughly

FIGURE 1.2   **WORLD POPULATION BY GDP PER WORKER, 1960 AND 1988**

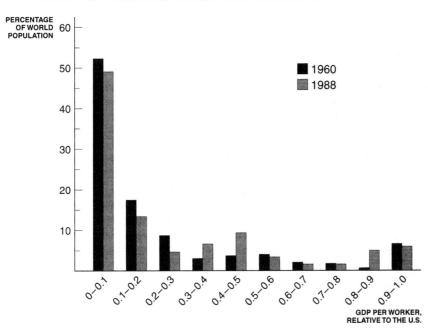

SOURCE: Penn World Tables Mark 5.6, Summers and Heston (1991).
   Note: The sample size has been reduced to 121 countries in order to incorporate the 1960 data.

the equivalent of Japan, well below the other industrialized economies. Singapore, on the other hand, has a GDP per worker of $24,344, even higher than Japanese GDP per worker.

   An important characteristic of these NICs is their extremely rapid rates of growth, and this leads to our next fact:

FACT # 2   **Rates of economic growth vary substantially across countries.**

   The last two columns of Table 1.1 characterize economic growth. The fourth column reports the average annual change in the (natural) log of GDP per worker from 1960 to 1990.[8] Growth in GDP per worker in the United States averaged only 1.4 percent per year from 1960 to 1990. France, West Germany, and the United Kingdom grew a bit more rapidly, while Japan grew at a remarkable rate of 5.0 percent. The NICs exceeded even Japan's astounding rate of increase, truly exemplifying what is meant by the term "growth miracle." The poorest countries of the world exhibited varied growth performance. China and India, for example, grew faster than the United States from 1960 to 1990, but their growth rates were less than half those of the NICs. Other developing countries such as Zimbabwe and Uganda experienced little or no growth over the period. Finally, growth rates in a number of countries were negative from 1960 to 1990, earning these countries the label "growth disasters." Real incomes actually declined in countries such as Venezuela, Madagascar, and Chad, as shown in the last panel of Table 1.1.

A useful way to interpret these growth rates was provided by Robert E. Lucas, Jr. in a paper entitled "On the Mechanics of Economic Development" (1988). A convenient rule of thumb used by Lucas is that a country growing at g percent per year will double its per capita income every $70/g$ years.[9] According to this rule, U.S. GDP per worker will double approximately every 50 years, while Japanese GDP per worker will double approximately every 14 years. In other words, if these growth rates persisted for two generations, the average American or Indian would be two or three times as rich as his or her grandparents. The average citizen of Japan, Hong Kong, or South Korea would be *twenty* times as rich as his or her grandparents. Over moderate periods of time,

---

[8] See Appendix A for a discussion of how this concept of growth relates to percentage changes.

[9] Let $y(t)$ be per capita income at time t and let y_0 be some initial value of per capita income. Then $y(t) = y_0 e^{gt}$. The time it takes per capita income to double is given by the time t^* at which $y(t) = 2y_0$. Therefore,

$$2y_0 = y_0 e^{gt^*}$$

$$\Longrightarrow t^* = \frac{\log 2}{g}.$$

The rule of thumb is established by noting that $\log 2 \approx .7$. See Appendix A for further discussion.

small differences in growth rates can lead to enormous differences in per capita incomes.

FACT # 3   **Growth rates are not necessarily constant over time.**

In the United States and in many of the poorest countries of the world, growth rates have not changed much over the last century. On the other hand, growth rates have increased dramatically in countries such as Japan and the NICs. A simple way to see this is to note that a country growing at 5 percent per year with a per capita income of something like $10,000 cannot have been growing this rapidly forever. Per capita income will double every fourteen years at this rate, meaning that per capita income must have been below $250 within the last century. If we take this as a subsistence level of income, then clearly countries cannot have been growing at 5 percent per year for very long. By a similar argument, even the modest 2 percent growth of the industrialized countries cannot have been occurring forever. Growth rates must have increased at some point in the past.

Another way to see that growth rates are not always constant over time is to consider a few examples. India's average growth rate from 1960 to 1990 was 2.0 percent per year. From 1960 to 1980, however, its growth rate was only 1.3 percent per year; during the 1980s growth accelerated to 3.4 percent per year. Singapore did not experience particularly rapid growth until after the 1950s. The island country of Mauritius exhibited a strong *decline* in GDP per worker of 1.2 percent per year in the two decades following 1950. From 1970 to 1990, however, Mauritius grew at 3.6 percent per year. As a final example, according to several accounts China's annual growth rate has been nearly 10 percent in recent years. This rate seems too high to be taken at face value, but there is little doubt that the Chinese economy has recently experienced very rapid growth.

The substantial variation in growth rates both across and within countries leads to an important corollary of Facts 2 and 3. It is so important that we will call it a fact itself:

FACT # 4   **A country's relative position in the world distribution of per capita incomes is not immutable. Countries can move from being "poor" to being "rich," and vice-versa.**[10]

1.2 OTHER "STYLIZED FACTS"

Facts 1 through 4 apply broadly to the countries of the world. The next fact describes some features of the U.S. economy. These features turn out to be extremely important, as we will see in Chapter 2. They are general characteristics of most economies "in the long run."

FACT # 5   **In the United States over the last century,**

1. **the real rate of return to capital, r, shows no trend upward or downward;**

2. **the shares of income devoted to capital, rK/Y, and labor, wL/Y, show no trend; and**

3. **the average growth rate of output per person has been positive and relatively constant over time — i.e., the United States exhibits steady, sustained per capita income growth.**

This stylized fact, really a collection of facts, is drawn largely from a lecture given by Nicholas Kaldor at a 1958 conference on capital accu-

---

[10]A classic example of the latter is Argentina. At the end of the nineteenth century, Argentina was one of the richest countries in the world. With a tremendous natural resource base and a rapidly developing infrastructure, it attracted foreign investment and immigration on a large scale. By 1990, however, Argentina's per capita income was only about one-third of per capita income in the United States. Carlos Diaz-Alejandro (1970) provides a classic discussion of the economic history of Argentina.

mulation (Kaldor, 1961). Kaldor, following the advice of Charles Bab-
bage, began the lecture by claiming that the economic theorist should
begin with a summary of the "stylized" facts a theory was supposed to
explain.

Kaldor's first fact — that the rate of return to capital is roughly constant — is best seen by noting that the real interest rate on government
debt in the U.S. economy shows no trend. Granted, we do not observe
real interest rates, but one can take the nominal interest rate and sub-
tract off either the expected or the actual rate of inflation to make this
observation.

The second fact concerns payments to the factors of production,
which we can group into capital and labor. For the United States, one
can calculate labor's share of GDP by looking at wage and salary payments and compensation for the self-employed as a share of GDP.[11]
These calculations reveal that the labor share has been relatively constant over time, at a value of around 0.7. If we are focusing on a model
with two factors, and if we assume that there are no economic profits
in the model, then the capital share is simply 1 minus the labor share,
or 0.3. These first two facts imply that the capital-output ratio, K/Y, is
roughly constant in the United States.

The third fact is a slight reinterpretation of one of Kaldor's stylized
facts, illustrated in Figure 1.3. The figure plots per capita GDP (on a log
scale) for the United States from 1870 until 1994. The trend line in the
figure rises at a rate of 1.8 percent per year, and the relative constancy
of the growth rate can be seen by noting that apart from the ups and
downs of business cycles, this constant growth rate path "fits" the data
very well.

FACT # 6   **Growth in output and growth in the volume of international trade are closely related.**

Figure 1.4 documents the close relationship between the growth in a
country's output (GDP) and growth in its volume of trade. Here, the

[11] These data are reported in the National Income and Product Accounts. See, for example,
the Council of Economic Advisors (1997).

FIGURE 1.3   **REAL PER CAPITA GDP IN THE UNITED STATES, 1870—1994**

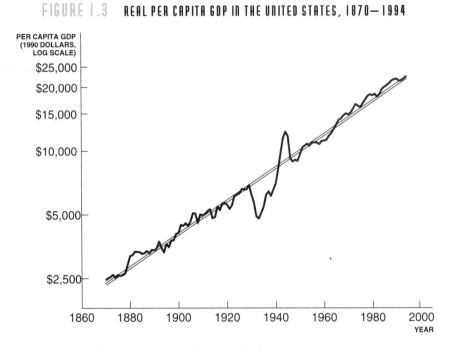

SOURCE: Maddison (1995) and author's calculations.

volume of trade is defined as the sum of exports and imports, but a similar figure could be produced with either component of trade. Notice that for many countries, trade volume has grown faster than GDP; the share of exports and imports in GDP has generally increased around the world since 1960.[12]

The relationship between trade and economic performance is complicated. Some economies, such as those of Hong Kong, Singapore, and Luxembourg, have flourished as regional "trade centers." The trade intensity ratio — the sum of exports and imports divided by GDP — for these economies *exceeds* 150 percent. How is this possible? These economies import unfinished products, add value by completing the

---

[12]On this point, it is interesting to note that the world economy was very open to international trade prior to World War I. Jeffrey Sachs and Andrew Warner (1995) argue that much of the trade liberalization since World War II, at least until the 1980s, simply re-establishes the global nature of markets that prevailed in 1900.

FIGURE 1.4   GROWTH IN TRADE AND GDP, 1960—90

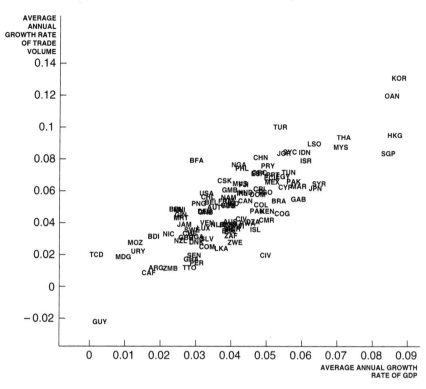

SOURCE: Penn World Tables Mark 5.6, Summers and Heston (1991).

production process, and then export the result. GDP, of course, is only generated in the second step. A substantial component of the strong growth performance turned in by these economies is associated with an increase in trade intensity.

On the other hand, trade intensity in Japan actually fell from around 21 percent in 1960 to around 18 percent in 1992 despite rapid per capita growth. And nearly all of the countries in sub-Saharan Africa have trade intensities higher than Japan's. A number of these countries also saw trade intensity increase from 1960 to 1990 while economic growth performance faltered.

FACT # 7 **Both skilled and unskilled workers tend to migrate from poor to rich countries or regions.**

Robert Lucas emphasized this stylized fact in his aforementioned article. Evidence for the fact can be seen in the presence of in-migration restrictions in rich countries. It is an important observation because these movements of labor, which presumably are often very costly, tell us something about real wages. The returns to both skilled and unskilled labor must be *higher* in high-income regions than in low-income regions. Otherwise, labor would not be willing to pay the high costs of migration. In terms of skilled labor, this raises an interesting puzzle. Presumably skilled labor is scarce in developing economies, and simple theories predict that factor returns are highest where factors are scarce. Why, then, doesn't skilled labor migrate from the United States to Zaire?

1.3 THE REMAINDER OF THIS BOOK

Three central questions of economic growth and development are examined in the remainder of this book.

The first question is the one asked at the beginning of this chapter: Why are we so rich and they so poor? It is a question about *levels* of development and the world distribution of per capita incomes. This topic is explored in Chapters 2 and 3 and then is revisited in Chapter 7.

The second question is, What is the engine of economic growth? How is it that economies experience sustained growth in output per worker over the course of a century or more? Why is it that the United States has grown at 1.8 percent per year since 1870? The answer to these questions is *technological progress*. Understanding why technological progress occurs and how a country such as the United States can exhibit sustained growth is the subject of Chapters 4 and 5.

The final question concerns *growth miracles*. How is it that economies such as Japan's after World War II and those of Hong Kong, Singapore, and South Korea more recently are able to transform rapidly from "poor" to "rich?" Such Cinderella-like transformation gets at the heart of economic growth and development. Chapters 6 and 7 present one theory that integrates the models of the earlier chapters. Chapter 8 discusses alternative theories of economic growth, and Chapter 9 offers some conclusions.

Two appendices complete this book. Appendix A reviews the mathematics needed throughout the book.[13] Appendix B presents a collection of the data analyzed throughout the book. The country codes used in figures such as Figure 1.4 are also translated there.

The facts we have examined in this chapter indicate that it is not simply out of intellectual curiosity that we ask these questions. The answers hold the key to unlocking widespread rapid economic growth. Indeed, the recent experience of East Asia suggests that such growth has the power to transform standards of living over the course of a single generation. Surveying this evidence in the 1985 Marshall Lecture at Cambridge University, Robert E. Lucas, Jr., expressed the sentiment that fueled research on economic growth for the next decade:

> I do not see how one can look at figures like these without seeing them as representing *possibilities*. Is there some action a government of India could take that would lead the Indian economy to grow like Indonesia's or Egypt's? If so, *what* exactly? If not, what is it about the "nature of India" that makes it so? The consequences for human welfare involved in questions like these are simply staggering: Once one starts to think about them, it is hard to think about anything else (Lucas 1988, p. 5).

---

[13]Readers with a limited exposure to calculus, differential equations, and the mathematics of growth are encouraged to read Appendix A before continuing with the next chapter.

2 THE SOLOW MODEL

> All theory depends on assumptions which are not quite true. That is what makes it theory. The art of successful theorizing is to make the inevitable simplifying assumptions in such a way that the final results are not very sensitive. — Robert Solow (1956), p. 65.

In 1956, Robert Solow published a seminal paper on economic growth and development entitled "A Contribution to the Theory of Economic Growth." For this work and for his subsequent contributions to our understanding of economic growth, Solow was awarded the Nobel Prize in economics in 1987. In this chapter, we develop the model proposed by Solow and explore its ability to explain the stylized facts of growth and development discussed in Chapter 1. As we will see, this model provides an important cornerstone for understanding why some countries are vigorously rich while others are impoverished.

Following the advice of Solow in the quotation above, we will make several assumptions that may seem to be heroic. Nevertheless, we hope that these are simplifying assumptions in that, for the purposes at hand, they do not terribly distort the picture of the world we create. For example, the world we consider in this chapter will consist of countries that produce and consume only a single, homogeneous good (*output*). Conceptually, as well as for testing the model using empirical data, it is convenient to think of this output as units of a country's Gross Domestic Product, or GDP. One implication of this simplifying assumption is that there is no international trade in the model because there is only a single good: I'll give you a 1941 Joe DiMaggio autograph in exchange for . . . your 1941 Joe DiMaggio autograph? Another assumption of the model is that technology is *exogenous* — that is, the technology available to firms in this simple world is unaffected by the actions of the firms, including research and development (R&D). These are assumptions that we will relax later on, but for the moment, and for Solow, they serve well. Much progress in economics has been made by creating a very simple world and then seeing how it behaves and misbehaves.

Before presenting the Solow model, it is worth stepping back to consider exactly what a model is and what it is for. In modern economics, a model is a mathematical representation of some aspect of the economy. It is easiest to think of models as toy economies populated by robots. We specify exactly how the robots behave, which is typically to maximize their own utility. We also specify the constraints the robots face in seeking to maximize their utility. For example, the robots that populate our economy may want to consume as much output as possible, but they are limited by how much output they can produce given the techniques at their disposal. The best models are often very simple but convey enormous insight into how the world works. Consider the supply and demand framework in microeconomics. This basic tool is remarkably effective at predicting how the prices and quantities of goods as diverse as health care, computers, and nuclear weapons will respond to changes in the economic environment.

With this understanding of how and why economists develop models, we pause to highlight one of the important assumptions we will make until the final chapters of this book. Instead of writing down utility functions that the robots in our economy maximize, we will summarize the results of utility maximization with elementary rules that the robots obey. For example, a common problem in economics is for an individual to decide how much to consume today and how much to save for consumption in the future. Or for individuals to decide how much time to spend going to school to accumulate skills and how much time to spend working in the labor market. Instead of writing these problems down formally, we will assume that individuals save a constant fraction of their income and spend a constant fraction of their time accumulating skills. These are extremely useful simplifications; without them, the models are difficult to solve without more advanced mathematical techniques. For many purposes, these are fine assumptions to make in our first pass at understanding economic growth. Rest assured, however, that we will relax these assumptions in Chapter 7.

2.1 THE BASIC SOLOW MODEL

The Solow model is built around two equations, a production function and a capital accumulation equation. The production function describes how inputs such as bulldozers, semiconductors, engineers, and steelworkers combine to produce output. To simplify the model, we group these inputs into two categories, capital, K, and labor, L, and denote output as Y. The *production function* is assumed to have the Cobb-Douglas form and is given by

$$Y = F(K, L) = K^\alpha L^{1-\alpha}, \tag{2.1}$$

where α is some number between 0 and 1.[1] Notice that this production function exhibits *constant returns to scale:* if all of the inputs are doubled, output will exactly double.[2]

Firms in this economy pay workers a wage, w, for each unit of labor and pay r in order to rent a unit of capital for one period. We assume there are a large number of firms in the economy so that perfect competition prevails and the firms are price-takers.[3] Normalizing the price of output in our economy to unity, profit-maximizing firms solve the following problem:

$$\max_{K,L} F(K, L) - rK - wL.$$

According to the first-order conditions for this problem, firms will hire labor until the marginal product of labor is equal to the wage and will

[1] Charles Cobb and Paul Douglas (1928) proposed this functional form in their analysis of U.S. manufacturing. Interestingly, they argued that this production function, with a value for α of 1/4, fit the data very well without allowing for technological progress.

[2] Recall that if $F(aK, aL) = aY$ for any number $a > 1$, then we say that the production function exhibits constant returns to scale. If $F(aK, aL) > aY$, then the production function exhibits *increasing returns to scale*, and if the inequality is reversed the production function exhibits *decreasing returns to scale*.

[3] You may recall from microeconomics that with constant returns to scale the number of firms is indeterminate, i.e., not pinned down by the model.

rent capital until the marginal product of capital is equal to the rental price:

$$w = \frac{\partial F}{\partial L} = (1 - \alpha)\frac{Y}{L},$$

$$r = \frac{\partial F}{\partial K} = \alpha\frac{Y}{K}.$$

Notice that $wL + rK = Y$. That is, payments to the inputs ("factor payments") completely exhaust the value of output produced so that there are no economic profits to be earned. This important result is a general property of production functions with constant returns to scale.

Recall from Chapter 1 that the stylized facts we are typically interested in explaining involve output per worker or per capita output. With this interest in mind, we can rewrite the production function in equation (2.1) in terms of output per worker, $y \equiv Y/L$, and capital per worker, $k \equiv K/L$:

$$y = k^\alpha. \tag{2.2}$$

This production function is graphed in Figure 2.1. With more capital per worker, firms produce more output per worker. However, there are diminishing returns to capital per worker: each additional unit of capital

FIGURE 2.1   A COBB-DOUGLAS PRODUCTION FUNCTION

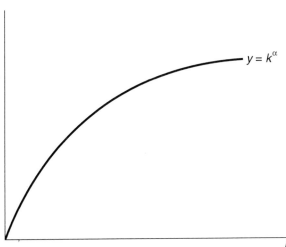

we give to a single worker increases the output of that worker by less and less.

The second key equation of the Solow model is an equation that describes how capital accumulates. The capital accumulation equation is given by

$$\dot{K} = sY - dK. \qquad (2.3)$$

This kind of equation will be used throughout this book and is very important, so let's pause a moment to explain carefully what this equation says. According to this equation, the change in the capital stock, $\dot{K}$, is equal to the amount of gross investment, sY, less the amount of depreciation that occurs during the production process, dK. We'll now discuss these three terms in more detail.

The term on the left-hand side of equation (2.3) is the continuous time version of $K_{t+1} - K_t$, that is, the change in the capital stock per "period." We use the "dot" notation[4] to denote a derivative with respect to time:

$$\dot{K} \equiv \frac{dK}{dt}.$$

The second term of equation (2.3) represents gross investment. Following Solow, we assume that workers/consumers save a constant fraction, s, of their combined wage and rental income, $Y = wL + rK$. The economy is closed, so that saving equals investment, and the only use of investment in this economy is to accumulate capital. The consumers then rent this capital to firms for use in production, as discussed above.

The third term of equation (2.3) reflects the depreciation of the capital stock that occurs during production. The standard functional form used here implies that a constant fraction, d, of the capital stock depreciates every period (regardless of how much output is produced). For example, we often assume $d = .05$, so that 5 percent of the machines and factories in our model economy wear out each year.

To study the evolution of output per person in this economy, we rewrite the capital accumulation equation in terms of capital per person. Then the production function in equation (2.2) will tell us the amount of output per person produced for whatever capital stock per person is present in the economy. This rewriting is most easily accomplished

[4] Appendix A discusses the meaning of this notation in more detail.

by using a simple mathematical trick that is often used in the study of growth. The mathematical trick is to "take logs and then derivatives" (see Appendix A for further discussion). Two examples of this trick are given below.

Example 1:

$$k \equiv K/L \Longrightarrow \log k = \log K - \log L$$

$$\Longrightarrow \frac{\dot{k}}{k} = \frac{\dot{K}}{K} - \frac{\dot{L}}{L}.$$

Example 2:

$$y = k^\alpha \Longrightarrow \log y = \alpha \log k$$

$$\Longrightarrow \frac{\dot{y}}{y} = \alpha \frac{\dot{k}}{k}.$$

Applying Example 1 to equation (2.3) will allow us to rewrite the capital accumulation equation in terms of capital per worker. But before we proceed, let's first consider the growth rate of the labor force, $\dot{L}/L$. An important assumption that will be maintained throughout most of this book is that the labor force participation rate is constant and that the population growth rate is given by the parameter n.[5] This implies that the labor force growth rate, $\dot{L}/L$, is also given by n. If $n = .01$, then the population and the labor force are growing at one percent per year. This exponential growth can be seen from the relationship

$$L(t) = L_0 e^{nt}.$$

Take logs and differentiate this equation, and what do you get?

Now we are ready to combine Example 1 and equation (2.3):

$$\frac{\dot{k}}{k} = \frac{sY}{K} - n - d$$

$$= \frac{sy}{k} - n - d.$$

This now yields the capital accumulation equation in per worker terms:

$$\dot{k} = sy - (n + d)k.$$

---

[5]Often, it is convenient in describing the model to assume the labor force participation rate is unity, i.e., every member of the population is also a worker.

This equation says that the change in capital per worker each period is determined by three terms. Two of the terms are analogous to the original capital accumulation equation. Investment per worker, sy, increases k, while depreciation per worker, dk, reduces k. The term that is new in this equation is a reduction in k because of population growth, the nk term. Each period, there are nL new workers around who were not there during the last period. If there were no new investment and no depreciation, capital *per worker* would decline because of the increase in the labor force. The amount by which it would decline is exactly nk, as can be seen by setting $\dot{K}$ to zero in Example 1.

2.1.1 THE SOLOW DIAGRAM

We've now derived the two key equations of the Solow model in terms of output per worker and capital per worker. These equations are

$$y = k^\alpha \tag{2.4}$$

and

$$\dot{k} = sy - (n + d)k. \tag{2.5}$$

Now we are ready to ask fundamental questions of our model. For example, an economy starts out with a given stock of capital per worker, k_0, and a given population growth rate, depreciation rate, and investment rate. How does output per worker evolve over time in this economy — i.e., how does the economy grow? How does output per worker compare in the long run between two economies that have different investment rates?

These questions are most easily analyzed in a Solow diagram, as shown in Figure 2.2. The Solow diagram consists of two curves, plotted as functions of the capital-labor ratio, k. The first curve is the amount of investment per person, $sy = sk^\alpha$. This curve has the same shape as the production function plotted in Figure 2.1, but it is translated down by the factor s. The second curve is the line $(n + d)k$, which represents the amount of new investment per person required to keep the amount of capital per worker constant — both depreciation and the growing workforce tend to reduce the amount of capital per person in the economy. By no coincidence, the difference between these two curves is the change in the amount of capital per worker. When this

FIGURE 2.2   THE BASIC SOLOW DIAGRAM

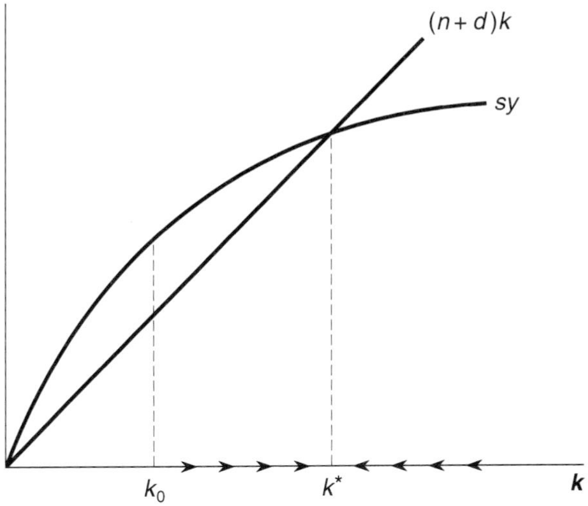

change is positive and the economy is increasing its capital per worker, we say that *capital deepening* is occuring. When this change is zero but the actual capital stock K is growing (because of population growth), we say that only *capital widening* is occurring.

To consider a specific example, suppose an economy has capital equal to the amount k_0 today, as drawn in Figure 2.2. What happens over time? At k_0, the amount of investment per worker exceeds the amount needed to keep capital per worker constant, so that capital deepening occurs — that is, k increases over time. This capital deepening will continue until $k = k^*$, at which point $sy = (n + d)k$, so that $\dot{k} = 0$. At this point, the amount of capital per worker remains constant, and we call such a point a *steady state*.

What would happen if instead the economy began with a capital stock per worker larger than k^*? At points to the right of k^* in Figure 2.2, the amount of investment per worker provided by the economy is less than the amount needed to keep the capital-labor ratio constant. The term $\dot{k}$ is negative, and therefore the amount of capital per worker begins to decline in this economy. This decline occurs until the amount of capital per worker falls to k^*.

Notice that the Solow diagram determines the steady-state value of capital per worker. The production function of equation (2.4) then

FIGURE 2.3   THE SOLOW DIAGRAM AND THE PRODUCTION FUNCTION

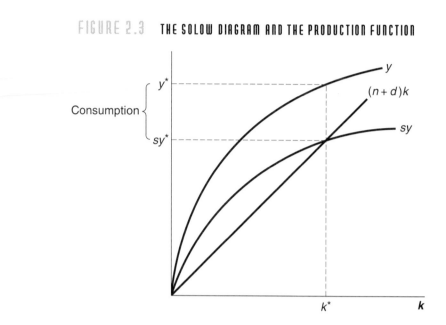

determines the steady-state value of output per worker, y^*, as a function of k^*. It is sometimes convenient to include the production function in the Solow diagram itself to make this point clearly. This is done in Figure 2.3. Notice that steady-state consumption per worker is then given by the difference between steady-state output per worker, y^*, and steady-state investment per worker, sy^*.

2.1.2 COMPARATIVE STATICS

Comparative statics are used to examine the response of the model to changes in the values of various parameters. In this section, we will consider what happens to per capita income in an economy that begins in steady state but then experiences a "shock." The shocks we will consider are an increase in the investment rate, s, and an increase in the population growth rate, n.

AN INCREASE IN THE INVESTMENT RATE   Consider an economy that has arrived at its steady-state value of output per worker. Now suppose that the consumers in that economy decide to increase the investment rate permanently from s to some value s'. What happens to k and y in this economy?

The answer is found in Figure 2.4. The increase in the investment rate shifts the *sy* curve upward to *s'y*. At the current value of the capital stock, k^*, investment per worker now exceeds the amount required to keep capital per worker constant, and therefore the economy begins capital deepening again. This capital deepening continues until $s'y = (n + d)k$ and the capital stock per worker reaches a higher value indicated by the point k^{**}. From the production function, we know that this higher level of capital per worker will be associated with higher per capita output; the economy is now richer than it was before.

AN INCREASE IN THE POPULATION GROWTH RATE   Now consider an alternative exercise. Suppose an economy has reached its steady state, but then because of immigration, for example, the population growth rate of the economy rises from *n* to *n'*. What happens to *k* and *y* in this economy?

Figure 2.5 computes the answer graphically. The $(n + d)k$ curve rotates up and to the left to the new curve $(n' + d)k$. At the current value of the capital stock k^*, investment per worker is now no longer high enough to keep the capital-labor ratio constant in the face of the rising population. Therefore the capital-labor ratio begins to fall. It continues to fall until the point at which $sy = (n' + d)k$, indicated by k^{**} in

FIGURE 2.4   AN INCREASE IN THE INVESTMENT RATE

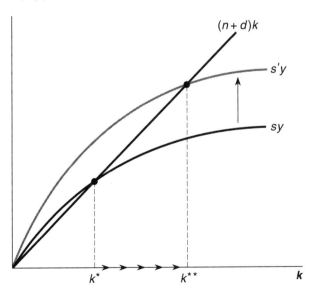

FIGURE 2.5 AN INCREASE IN POPULATION GROWTH

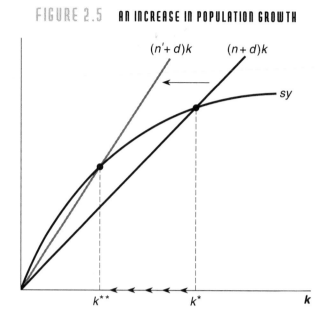

Figure 2.5. At this point, the economy has less capital per worker than it began with and is therefore poorer: per capita output is ultimately lower after the increase in population growth in this example. Why?

2.1.3 PROPERTIES OF THE STEADY STATE

By definition, the steady-state quantity of capital per worker is determined by the condition that $\dot{k} = 0$. Equations (2.4) and (2.5) allow us to use this condition to solve for the steady-state quantities of capital per worker and output per worker. Substituting from (2.4) into (2.5),

$$\dot{k} = sk^\alpha - (n + d)k,$$

and setting this equation equal to zero yields

$$k^* = \left(\frac{s}{n + d}\right)^{1/(1-\alpha)}.$$

Substituting this into the production function reveals the steady-state quantity of output per worker, y^*:

$$y^* = \left(\frac{s}{n + d}\right)^{\alpha/(1-\alpha)}.$$

This equation reveals the Solow model's answer to the question "Why are we so rich and they so poor?" Countries that have high savings/investment rates will tend to be richer, *ceteris paribus*.[6] Such countries accumulate more capital per worker, and countries with more capital per worker have more output per worker. Countries that have high population growth rates, in contrast, will tend to be poorer, according to the Solow model. A higher fraction of savings in these economies must go simply to keep the capital-labor ratio constant in the face of a growing population. This capital-widening requirement makes capital deepening more difficult and these economies tend to accumulate less capital per worker.

How well do these predictions of the Solow model hold up empirically? Figures 2.6 and 2.7 plot GDP per worker against gross investment

FIGURE 2.6   GDP PER WORKER VERSUS INVESTMENT RATES

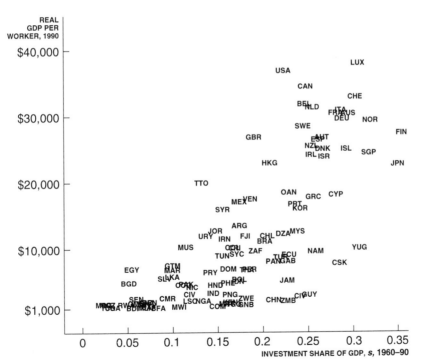

---

[6] *Ceteris paribus* is Latin for "all other things being equal."

FIGURE 2.7   GDP PER WORKER VERSUS POPULATION GROWTH RATES

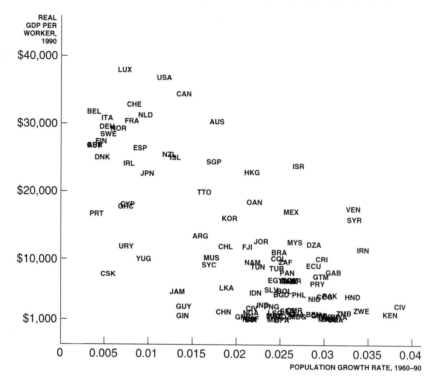

as a share of GDP and against population growth rates, respectively. Broadly speaking, the predictions of the Solow model are borne out by the empirical evidence. Countries with high investment rates tend to be richer on average than countries with low investment rates, and countries with high population growth rates tend to be poorer on average. At this level, then, the general predictions of the Solow model seem to be supported by the data.

2.1.4 ECONOMIC GROWTH IN THE SIMPLE MODEL

What does economic growth look like in the steady state of this simple version of the Solow model? The answer is that there is *no* per capita growth in this version of the model! Output per worker (and therefore per person, since we've assumed the labor force participation rate is constant) is constant in the steady state. Output itself, Y, is growing, of course, but only at the rate of population growth.[7]

This version of the model fits several of the stylized facts discussed in Chapter 1. It generates differences in per capita income across countries. It generates a constant capital-output ratio (because both k and y are constant, implying that K/Y is constant). It generates a constant interest rate, the marginal product of capital. However, it fails to predict a very important stylized fact: that economies exhibit sustained per capita income growth. In this model, economies may grow for a while, but not forever. For example, an economy that begins with a stock of capital per worker below its steady-state value will experience growth in k and y along the *transition path* to the steady state. Over time, however, growth slows down as the economy approaches its steady state, and eventually growth stops altogether.

To see that growth slows down along the transition path, notice two things. First, from the capital accumulation equation,

$$\frac{\dot{k}}{k} = sk^{\alpha-1} - (n+d). \tag{2.6}$$

Because α is less than one, as k rises, the growth rate of k gradually declines. Second, from Example 2, the growth rate of y is proportional to the growth rate of k, so that the same statement holds true for output per worker.

The transition dynamics implied by equation (2.6) are plotted in Figure 2.8.[8] The first term on the right-hand side of the equation is $sk^{\alpha-1}$, which is equal to sy/k. The higher the level of capital per worker, the lower the average product of capital y/k, because of diminishing returns to capital accumulation (α is less than one). Therefore, this curve slopes downward. The second term on the right-hand side of equation (2.6) is $n+d$, which doesn't depend on k, so it is plotted as a horizontal line. The difference between the two lines in Figure 2.8

---

[7] This can be seen easily by applying the "take logs and differentiate" trick to $y \equiv Y/L$.
[8] This alternative version of the Solow diagram makes the growth implications of the Solow model much more transparent. Xavier Sala-i-Martin (1990) emphasizes this point.

FIGURE 2.8   TRANSITION DYNAMICS

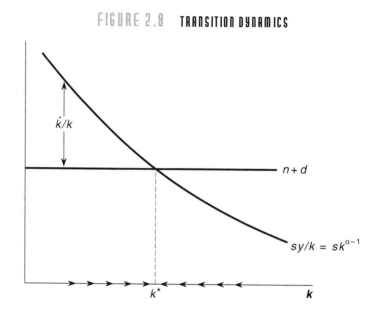

is the growth rate of the capital stock, or $\dot{k}/k$. Thus, the figure clearly indicates that the further an economy is below its steady-state value of k, the faster the economy grows. Also, the further an economy is above its steady-state value of k, the faster k declines.

2.2 TECHNOLOGY AND THE SOLOW MODEL

To generate sustained growth in per capita income in this model, we must follow Solow and introduce technological progress to the model. This is accomplished by adding a technology variable, A, to the production function:

$$Y = F(K, AL) = K^\alpha (AL)^{1-\alpha}. \tag{2.7}$$

Entered this way, the technology variable A is said to be "labor-augmenting" or "Harrod-neutral."[9] Technological progress occurs when

[9]The other possibilities are $F(AK, L)$, which is known as "capital-augmenting" or "Solow-neutral" technology, and $AF(K, L)$, which is known as "Hicks-neutral" technology. With the Cobb-Douglas functional form assumed here, this distinction is less important.

A increases over time — a unit of labor, for example, is more productive when the level of technology is higher.

An important assumption of the Solow model is that technological progress is *exogenous*: in a common phrase, technology is like "manna from heaven," in that it descends upon the economy automatically and regardless of whatever else is going on in the economy. Instead of modeling carefully where technology comes from, we simply recognize for the moment that there is technological progress and make the assumption that A is growing at a constant rate:

$$\frac{\dot{A}}{A} = g \Longleftrightarrow A = A_0 e^{gt},$$

where g is a parameter representing the growth rate of technology. Of course, this assumption about technology is unrealistic, and explaining how to relax this assumption is one of the major accomplishments of the "new" growth theory that we will explore in later chapters.

The capital accumulation equation in the Solow model with technology is the same as before. Rewriting it slightly, we get

$$\frac{\dot{K}}{K} = s\frac{Y}{K} - d. \tag{2.8}$$

To see the growth implications of the model with technology, first rewrite the production function (2.7) in terms of output per worker:

$$y = k^\alpha A^{1-\alpha}.$$

Then take logs and differentiate:

$$\frac{\dot{y}}{y} = \alpha\frac{\dot{k}}{k} + (1-\alpha)\frac{\dot{A}}{A}. \tag{2.9}$$

Finally, notice from the capital accumulation equation (2.8) that the growth rate of K will be constant if and only if Y/K is constant. Furthermore, if Y/K is constant, y/k is also constant, and most importantly, y and k will be growing at the same rate. A situation in which capital, output, consumption, and population are growing at constant rates is called a *balanced growth path*. Partly because of its empirical appeal, this is a situation that we often wish to analyze in our models. For example, according to Fact 5 in Chapter 1, this situation describes the U.S. economy.

Let's use the notation g_x to denote the growth rate of some variable x along a balanced growth path. Then, along a balanced growth path, $g_y = g_k$ according to the argument above. Substituting this relationship into equation (2.9) and recalling that $\dot{A}/A = g$,

$$g_y = g_k = g. \qquad (2.10)$$

That is, along a balanced growth path in the Solow model, output per worker and capital per worker both grow at the rate of exogenous technological change, g. Notice that in the model of Section 2.1, there was no technological progress, and therefore there was no long-run growth in output per worker or capital per worker; $g_y = g_k = g = 0$. The model with technology reveals that *technological progress is the source of sustained per capita growth*. In this chapter, this result is little more than an assumption; in later chapters, we will explore the result in much more detail and come to the same conclusion.

2.2. THE SOLOW DIAGRAM WITH TECHNOLOGY

The analysis of the Solow model with technological progress proceeds very much like the analysis in Section 2.1: we set up a differential equation and analyze it in a Solow diagram to find the steady state. The only important difference is that the variable k is no longer constant in the long run, so we have to write our differential equation in terms of another variable. The new *state* variable will be $\tilde{k} \equiv K/AL$. Notice that this is equivalent to k/A and is obviously constant along the balanced growth path because $g_k = g_A = g$. The variable $\tilde{k}$ therefore represents the ratio of capital per worker to technology. We will refer to this as the "capital-technology" ratio (keeping in mind that the numerator is capital per worker rather than the total level of capital).

Rewriting the production function in terms of $\tilde{k}$, we get

$$\tilde{y} = \tilde{k}^{\alpha}, \qquad (2.11)$$

where $\tilde{y} \equiv Y/AL = y/A$. Following the terminology above, we will refer to $\tilde{y}$ as the "output-technology ratio."[10]

---

[10]The variables $\tilde{y}$ and $\tilde{k}$ are sometimes referred to as "output per effective unit of labor" and "capital per effective unit of labor." This labeling is motivated by the fact that technological progress is labor-augmenting. AL is then the "effective" amount of labor used in production.

Rewriting the capital accumulation equation in terms of $\tilde{k}$ is accomplished by following exactly the methodology used in Section 2.1. First, note that

$$\frac{\dot{\tilde{k}}}{\tilde{k}} = \frac{\dot{K}}{K} - \frac{\dot{A}}{A} - \frac{\dot{L}}{L}.$$

Combining this with the capital accumulation equation reveals that

$$\dot{\tilde{k}} = s\tilde{y} - (n + g + d)\tilde{k}. \tag{2.12}$$

The similarity of equations (2.11) and (2.12) to their counterparts in Section 2.1 should be obvious.

The Solow diagram with technological progress is presented in Figure 2.9. The analysis of this diagram is very similar to the analysis when there is no technological progress, but the interpretation is slightly different. If the economy begins with a capital-technology ratio that is below its steady-state level, say at a point such as $\tilde{k}_0$, the capital-technology ratio will rise gradually over time. Why? Because the amount of investment being undertaken exceeds the amount needed to keep the capital-technology ratio constant. This will be true until $s\tilde{y} = (n+g+d)\tilde{k}$ at the point $\tilde{k}^*$, at which point the economy is in steady state and grows along a balanced growth path.

FIGURE 2.9   THE SOLOW DIAGRAM WITH TECHNOLOGICAL PROGRESS

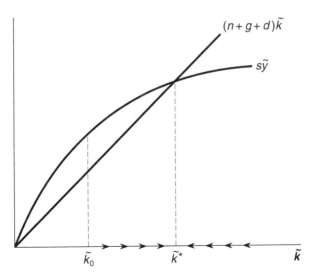

2.2.2 SOLVING FOR THE STEADY STATE

The steady-state output-technology ratio is determined by the production function and the condition that $\dot{\tilde{k}} = 0$. Solving for $\tilde{k}^*$, we find that

$$\tilde{k}^* = \left(\frac{s}{n+g+d}\right)^{1/(1-\alpha)}.$$

Substituting this into the production function yields

$$\tilde{y}^* = \left(\frac{s}{n+g+d}\right)^{\alpha/(1-\alpha)}.$$

To see what this implies about output per worker, rewrite the equation as

$$y^*(t) = A(t)\left(\frac{s}{n+g+d}\right)^{\alpha/(1-\alpha)}, \qquad (2.13)$$

where we explicitly note the dependence of y and A on time. From equation (2.13), we see that output per worker along the balanced growth path is determined by technology, the investment rate, and the population growth rate. For the special case of $g = 0$ and $A_0 = 1$ — i.e., of no technological progress — this result is identical to that derived in Section 2.1.

An interesting result is apparent from equation (2.13) and is discussed in more detail in Exercise 2 at the end of this chapter. That is, changes in the investment rate or the population growth rate affect the long-run *level* of output per worker but do not affect the long-run *growth rate* of output per worker. To see this more clearly, let's consider a simple example.

Suppose an economy begins in steady state with investment rate s and then permanently increases its investment rate to s' (for example, because of a permanent subsidy to investment). The Solow diagram for this policy change is drawn in Figure 2.10, and the results are broadly similar to the case with no technological progress. At the initial capital-technology ratio $\tilde{k}^*$, investment exceeds the amount needed to keep the capital-technology ratio constant, so $\tilde{k}$ begins to rise.

FIGURE 2.10   AN INCREASE IN THE INVESTMENT RATE

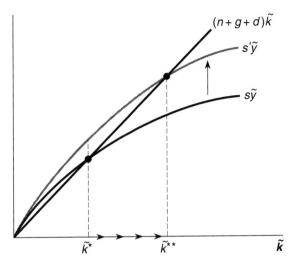

To see the effects on growth, rewrite equation (2.12) as

$$\frac{\dot{\tilde{k}}}{\tilde{k}} = s\frac{\tilde{y}}{\tilde{k}} - (n + g + d),$$

and note that $\tilde{y}/\tilde{k}$ is equal to $\tilde{k}^{\alpha-1}$. Figure 2.11 illustrates the transition dynamics implied by this equation. As the diagram shows, the increase in the investment rate to s' raises the growth rate temporarily as the economy transits to the new steady state, $\tilde{k}^{**}$. Since g is constant, faster growth in $\tilde{k}$ along the transition path implies that output per worker increases more rapidly than technology: $\dot{y}/y > g$. The behavior of the growth rate of output per worker over time is displayed in Figure 2.12.

Figure 2.13 cumulates the effects on growth to show what happens to the (log) level of output per worker over time. Prior to the policy change, output per worker is growing at the constant rate g, so that the log of output per worker rises linearly. At the time of the policy change, t^*, output per worker begins to grow more rapidly. This more rapid growth continues temporarily until the output-technology ratio reaches its new steady state. At this point, growth has returned to its long-run level of g.

FIGURE 2.11   AN INCREASE IN THE INVESTMENT RATE: TRANSITION DYNAMICS

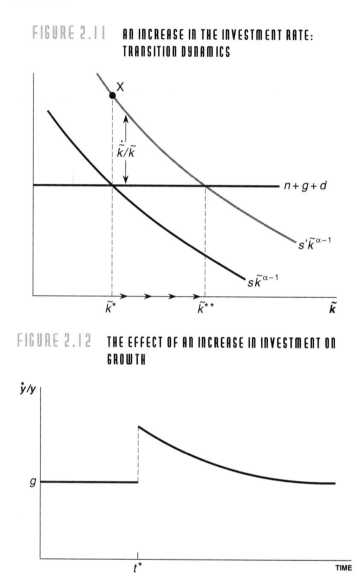

FIGURE 2.12   THE EFFECT OF AN INCREASE IN INVESTMENT ON GROWTH

This exercise illustrates two important points. First, policy changes in the Solow model increase growth rates, but only temporarily along the transition to the new steady state. That is, policy changes have no long-run *growth effect*. Second, policy changes can have *level effects*. That is, a permanent policy change can permanently raise (or lower) the level of per capita output.

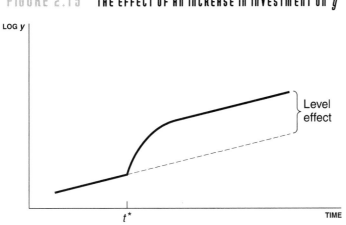

FIGURE 2.13   THE EFFECT OF AN INCREASE IN INVESTMENT ON y

2.3 EVALUATING THE SOLOW MODEL

How does the Solow model answer the key questions of growth and development? First, the Solow model appeals to differences in investment rates and population growth rates and (perhaps) to exogenous differences in technology to explain differences in per capita incomes. Why are we so rich and they so poor? According to the Solow model, it is because we invest more and have lower population growth rates, both of which allow us to accumulate more capital per worker and thus increase labor productivity. In the next chapter, we will explore this hypothesis more carefully and see that it is firmly supported by data across the countries of the world.

Second, why do economies exhibit sustained growth in the Solow model? The answer is technological progress. As we saw earlier, without technological progress, per capita growth will eventually cease as diminishing returns to capital set in. Technological progress, however, can offset the tendency for the marginal product of capital to fall, and in the long run, countries exhibit per capita growth at the rate of technological progress.

How, then, does the Solow model account for differences in growth rates across countries? At first glance, it may seem that the Solow model cannot do so, except by appealing to differences in (unmodeled) technological progress. A more subtle explanation, however, can be found

by appealing to transition dynamics. We have seen several examples
of how transition dynamics can allow countries to grow at rates different from their long-run growth rates. For example, an economy with a
capital-technology ratio below its long-run level will grow rapidly until
the capital-technology ratio reaches its steady-state level. This reasoning may help explain why countries such as Japan and Germany, which
had their capital stocks wiped out by World War II, have grown more
rapidly than the United States over the last fifty years. Or it may explain
why an economy that increases its investment rate will grow rapidly as
it makes the transition to a higher output-technology ratio. This explanation may work well for countries such as South Korea, Singapore, and
Taiwan. Their investment rates have increased dramatically since 1950,
as shown in Figure 2.14. The explanation may work less well, however,
for an economy such as Hong Kong's. This kind of reasoning raises an
interesting question: can countries permanently grow at different rates?
This question will be discussed in more detail in later chapters.

FIGURE 2.14   INVESTMENT RATES IN SOME NEWLY INDUSTRIALIZING
ECONOMIES

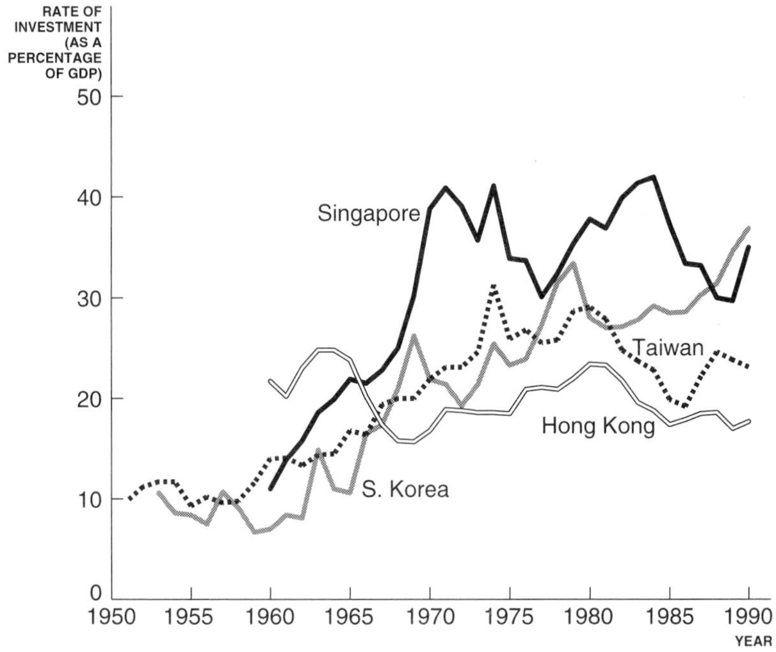

2.4 GROWTH ACCOUNTING AND THE PRODUCTIVITY SLOWDOWN

We have seen in the Solow model that sustained growth occurs only in the presence of technological progress. Without technological progress, capital accumulation runs into diminishing returns. With technological progress, however, improvements in technology continually offset the diminishing returns to capital accumulation. Labor productivity grows as a result, both directly because of the improvements in technology and indirectly because of the additional capital accumulation these improvements make possible.

In 1957, Solow published a second article, "Technical Change and the Aggregate Production Function," in which he performed a simple accounting exercise to break down growth in output into growth in capital, growth in labor, and growth in technological change. This "growth-accounting" exercise begins by postulating a production function such as

$$Y = BK^{\alpha}L^{1-\alpha},$$

where B is a Hicks-neutral productivity term.[11] Taking logs and differentiating this production function, one derives the key formula of growth accounting:

$$\frac{\dot{Y}}{Y} = \alpha \frac{\dot{K}}{K} + (1 - \alpha)\frac{\dot{L}}{L} + \frac{\dot{B}}{B}. \tag{2.14}$$

This equation says that output growth is equal to a weighted average of capital and labor growth plus the growth rate of B. This last term, $\dot{B}/B$, is commonly referred to as *total factor productivity growth* or *multifactor productivity growth*. Solow, as well as economists such as Edward Denison and Dale Jorgenson who followed Solow's approach, have used this equation to understand the sources of growth in output.

Using data on output, capital, and labor, and choosing a value of $\alpha = 1/3$ to match the factor income share for capital, a simple growth-accounting calculation is carried out in Table 2.1. The last line of the table reveals that growth in GDP for the United States from 1960 to 1990 averaged 3.1 percent per year. Slightly less than one percentage point

[11] In fact, this growth accounting can be done with a much more general production function such as $B(t)F(K, L)$, and the results are very similar.

TABLE 2.1   GROWTH ACCOUNTING FOR THE UNITED STATES

	Growth rate of GDP	Growth rate contributions of			Growth rate of GDP per worker
		Capital	Labor	TFP	
1960–70	4.0	0.8	1.2	1.9	2.2
1970–80	2.7	0.9	1.5	0.2	0.4
1980–90	2.6	0.8	0.7	1.0	1.5
1960–90	3.1	0.9	1.2	1.1	1.4

SOURCE: Penn World Tables Mark 5.6, an update of Summers and Heston (1991), and author's calculations.

Note: The table reports the average annual growth rate of GDP, together with the contributions due to capital, labor, and total factor productivity, following equation (2.14). A value of $\alpha = 1/3$ is used in the calculations. The last column reports the growth rate of GDP per worker for comparison.

of that growth was due to capital accumulation, 1.2 percent was due to growth in the labor force, and the remaining 1.1 percent is unexplained by growth in inputs to the production function. Because of the way it is calculated, economists have referred to this 1.1 percent as the "residual" or even as a "measure of our ignorance." One interpretation of this total factor productivity (TFP) growth term is that it is due to technological change; notice that in terms of the production function in equation (2.7), $B = A^{1-\alpha}$. This interpretation will be explored in later chapters.

Table 2.1 also reveals how GDP growth and its sources have changed over time in the United States. One of the important stylized facts revealed in the table is the productivity growth slowdown that occurred in the 1970s. The last column shows that growth in GDP per worker (or labor productivity) slowed dramatically in the 1970s — to 0.4 percent per year after the rapid growth of 2.2 percent per year during the 1960s. During the 1980s there was a partial recovery to 1.5 percent per year. What was the source of this slowdown in growth? Interestingly, the growth of the capital stock has been relatively constant over the entire thirty-year period; it even increased slightly during the 1970s. The labor force grew slightly faster in the 1970s, tending to reduce the growth of GDP per worker, but the primary culprit of the productivity slowdown is a substantial decline in the growth rate of TFP. For some reason, the "residual" was much lower during the 1970s than in the 1960s, and did not recover to its earlier level during the 1980s: the bulk of the productivity slowdown is accounted for by the "measure of our ignorance." A similar productivity slowdown occurred throughout the advanced countries of the world at about the same time.

Various explanations for the productivity slowdown have been advanced. For example, perhaps the sharp rise in energy prices in 1973 and 1979 contributed to the slowdown. One problem with this explanation is that in real terms energy prices were lower in the late 1980s than they were before the oil shocks. Another explanation may involve the changing composition of the labor force or the sectoral shift in the economy away from manufacturing (which tends to have high labor productivity) toward services (many of which have low labor productivity). This explanation receives some support from recent evidence that productivity growth recovered substantially in the 1980s in manufacturing. It is possible that a slowdown in resources spent on research and development (R&D) in the late 1960s contributed to the slowdown as well. Or, perhaps it is not the 1970s and 1980s that need to be explained but rather the 1950s and 1960s: growth may simply have been artificially and temporarily high in the years following World War II because of the application to the private sector of new technologies created for the war. Finally, and somewhat ironically, a number of economists point to the information-technology revolution associated with the widespread application of computers. According to this hypothesis, growth has slowed temporarily while the economy adapts to high-tech production methods, and a productivity *boom* lies on the horizon.[12] Nevertheless, careful work on the productivity slowdown has failed to provide a complete explanation.[13]

Growth accounting has also been used to analyze economic growth in countries other than the United States. One of the more interesting applications is to the NICs of South Korea, Hong Kong, Singapore, and Taiwan. Recall from Chapter 1 that average annual growth rates

---

[12] See Paul David (1990) and Jeremy Greenwood and Mehmet Yorukoglu (1997).

[13] The fall 1988 issue of the *Journal of Economic Perspectives* contains several papers discussing potential explanations of the productivity slowdown.

exceeded five percent in these economies from 1960 to 1990. Alwyn Young (1995) shows that a large part of this growth is the result of factor accumulation: increases in investment in physical capital and education, increases in labor force participation, and a shift from agriculture into manufacturing. Support for Young's result is provided in Figure 2.15. The vertical axis measures growth in output per worker, while the horizontal axis measures growth in Harrod-neutral (i.e., labor augmenting) total factor productivity. That is, instead of focusing on growth in B, where $B = A^{1-\alpha}$, we focus on the growth of A. This change of variables is often convenient because along a steady-state balanced growth path, $g_y = g_A$. Countries growing along a balanced growth path, then, should lie on the 45-degree line in the figure.

Two features of Figure 2.15 stand out. First, while the growth rates of output per worker in the East Asian countries are clearly remarkable,

FIGURE 2.15   GROWTH ACCOUNTING

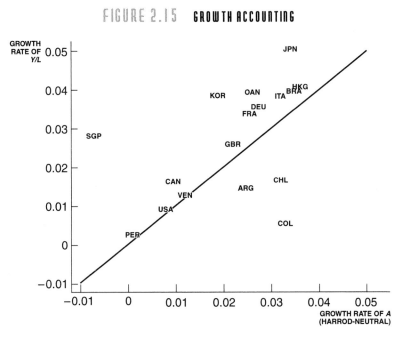

SOURCE: Author's calculations using the data collection reported in Table 10.8 of Barro and Sala-i-Martin (1995).

Note: The years over which growth rates are calculated vary across countries: 1960–90 for OECD, 1940–80 for Latin America, and 1966–90 for East Asia.

their TFP growth rates are less so. A number of other countries such as Italy, Brazil, and Chile have also experienced rapid TFP growth. Total factor productivity growth, while typically higher than in the United States, was not exceptional in the East Asian economies. Second, the East Asian countries are far above the 45-degree line. This shift means that growth in output per worker is much higher than TFP growth would suggest. Singapore is an extreme example, with slightly *negative* TFP growth. Its rapid growth of output per worker is entirely attributable to growth in capital and education. More generally, a key source of the rapid growth performance of these countries is factor accumulation. Therefore, Young concludes, the framework of the Solow model (and the extension of the model in Chapter 3) can explain a substantial amount of the rapid growth of the East Asian economies.

EXERCISES

1. *An increase in the labor force.* Shocks to an economy, such as wars, famines, or the unification of two economies, often generate large one-time flows of workers across borders. What are the short-run and long-run effects on an economy of a one-time permanent increase in the stock of labor? Examine this question in the context of the Solow model with $g = 0$ and $n > 0$.

2. *A decrease in the investment rate.* Suppose the U.S. Congress enacts legislation that discourages saving and investment, such as the elimination of the investment tax credit that occurred in 1990. As a result, suppose the investment rate falls permanently from s' to s''. Examine this policy change in the Solow model with technological progress, assuming that the economy begins in steady state. Sketch a graph of how (the natural log of) output per worker evolves over time with and without the policy change. Make a similar graph for the growth rate of output per worker. Does the policy change permanently reduce the *level* or the *growth rate* of output per worker?

3. *An income tax.* Suppose the U.S. Congress decides to levy an income tax on both wage income and capital income. Instead of receiving $wL + rK = Y$, consumers receive $(1 - \tau)wL + (1 - \tau)rK = (1 - \tau)Y$.

Trace the consequences of this tax for output per worker in the short and long runs, starting from steady state.

4. *Manna falls faster.* Suppose that there is a permanent increase in the rate of technological progress so that g rises to g'. Sketch a graph of the growth rate of output per worker over time. Be sure to pay close attention to the transition dynamics.

5. *Can we save too much?* Consumption is equal to output minus investment: $c = (1 - s)y$. In the context of the Solow model with no technological progress, what is the savings rate that maximizes steady-state consumption per worker? What is the marginal product of capital in this steady state? Show this point in a Solow diagram. Be sure to draw the production function on the diagram, and show consumption and saving and a line indicating the marginal product of capital. Can we save too much?

6. *Solow (1956) versus Solow (1957).* In the Solow model, with $g = 0$, consider a one-time improvement in the level of technology, A. Specifically, suppose that $\log A$ rises by one unit. (Notice that this means that the level of technology is roughly doubled; to be exact, it has increased by a factor of 2.7, which is the approximate value of e.)

   (a) Using equation (2.13), by how much does output per worker increase in the long-run?

   (b) Starting with equation (2.14), perform the growth accounting implied by this exercise. How much of the increase in output per worker is due to a change in capital per worker, and how much is due to a change in total factor productivity?

   (c) In what sense does the growth-accounting result in part (b) produce a misleading picture of this experiment?

3 EMPIRICAL APPLICATIONS OF NEOCLASSICAL GROWTH MODELS

This chapter considers several applications of the Solow model and its descendents, which we will group together under the rubric of "neoclassical growth models." In the first section of this chapter, we develop one of the key descendents of the Solow model, an extension that incorporates human capital. Then, we examine the "fit" of the model. How well does the neoclassical growth model explain why some countries are rich and others are poor? In the second section of this chapter, we examine the model's predictions concerning growth rates and discuss the presence or lack of "convergence" in the data. Finally, the third section of this chapter merges the discussion of the cross-country distribution of income levels with the convergence literature and examines the future evolution of the world income distribution.

3.1 THE SOLOW MODEL WITH HUMAN CAPITAL

In an influential paper published in 1992, "A Contribution to the Empirics of Economic Growth," Gregory Mankiw, David Romer, and David Weil evaluated the empirical implications of the Solow model and concluded that it performed very well. They then noted that the "fit" of the model could be improved even more by extending the model to include human capital — that is, by recognizing that labor in different economies may possess different levels of education and different skills. Extending the Solow model to include human capital or skilled labor is relatively straightforward, as we shall see in this section.[1]

Suppose that output, Y, in an economy is produced by combining physical capital, K, with skilled labor, H, according to a constant-returns, Cobb-Douglas production function

$$Y = K^\alpha (AH)^{1-\alpha}, \tag{3.1}$$

where A represents labor-augmenting technology that grows exogenously at rate g.

Individuals in this economy accumulate human capital by spending time learning new skills instead of working. Let u denote the fraction of an individual's time spent learning skills, and let L denote the total amount of (raw) labor used in production in the economy.[2] We assume that unskilled labor learning skills for time u generates skilled labor H according to

$$H = e^{\psi u} L, \tag{3.2}$$

where ψ is a positive constant we will discuss in a moment. Notice that if $u = 0$, then $H = L$ — that is, all labor is unskilled. By increasing u, a unit of unskilled labor increases the *effective* units of skilled labor H. To see by how much, take logs and derivatives of equation (3.2) to see that

$$\frac{d \log H}{du} = \psi. \tag{3.3}$$

This equation states that a small increase in u increases H by the *percentage* ψ (or more correctly, $\psi \times 100$). The fact that the effects are

---

[1]The development here differs from that in Mankiw, Romer and Weil (1992) in one important way. Mankiw, Romer, and Weil allow an economy to accumulate human capital in the same way that it accumulates physical capital: by foregoing consumption. Here, instead, we follow Lucas (1988) in assuming that individuals spend time accumulating skills, much like a student going to school. See Exercise 5 at the end of this chapter.

[2]Notice that if P denotes the total population of the economy, then the total amount of labor input in the economy is given by $L \equiv (1 - u)P$.

proportional is driven by the somewhat odd presence of the exponential e in the equation. This formulation is intended to match a large literature in labor economics that finds that an additional year of schooling increases the wages earned by an individual by something like 10 percent.[3]

Physical capital is accumulated by investing some output instead of consuming it, as in Chapter 2:

$$\dot{K} = s_K Y - dK \qquad (3.4)$$

where s_K is the investment rate for physical capital and d is the constant depreciation rate.

We solve this model using the same techniques employed in Chapter 2. First, we let lower-case letters denote variables divided by the stock of unskilled labor, L, and rewrite the production function in terms of output per worker as

$$y = k^\alpha (Ah)^{1-\alpha}. \qquad (3.5)$$

Notice that $h = e^{\psi u}$. How do agents decide how much time to spend accumulating skills instead of working? Just as we assume that individuals save and invest a constant fraction of their income, we will assume that u is constant and given exogenously.[4]

The fact that h is constant means that the production function in equation (3.5) is very similar to that used in Chapter 2. In particular, along a balanced growth path, y and k will grow at the constant rate g, the rate of technological progress.

As in Chapter 2, the model is solved by considering "state variables" that are constant along a balanced growth path. There, recall that the state variables were terms such as y/A. Here, since h is constant, we can define the state variables by dividing by Ah. Denoting these state variables with a tilde, equation (3.5) implies that

$$\tilde{y} = \tilde{k}^\alpha, \qquad (3.6)$$

which is essentially the same as equation (2.11).

---

[3]Bils and Klenow (1996) apply this Mincerian formulation in the context of economic growth.

[4]We return to this issue in Chapter 7.

Following the reasoning in Chapter 2, the capital accumulation equation can be written in terms of the state variables as

$$\dot{\tilde{k}} = s_K \tilde{y} - (n + g + d)\tilde{k}. \tag{3.7}$$

Notice that in terms of state variables, this model is identical to the model we have already solved in Chapter 2. That is, equations (3.6) and (3.7) are identical to equations (2.11) and (2.12). This means that all of the results we discussed in Chapter 2 regarding the dynamics of the Solow model apply here. Adding human capital as we have done it does not change the basic flavor of the model.

The steady state values of $\tilde{k}$ and $\tilde{y}$ are found by setting $\dot{\tilde{k}} = 0$, which yields

$$\frac{\tilde{k}}{\tilde{y}} = \frac{s_K}{n + g + d}.$$

Substituting this condition into the production function in equation (3.6), we find the steady-state value of the output-technology ratio $\tilde{y}$:

$$\tilde{y}^* = \left(\frac{s_K}{n + g + d} \right)^{\alpha/(1-\alpha)}.$$

Rewriting this in terms of output per worker, we get

$$y^*(t) = \left(\frac{s_K}{n + g + d} \right)^{\alpha/(1-\alpha)} hA(t), \tag{3.8}$$

where we have explicitly included t to remind us which variables are growing over time.

This last equation summarizes the explanation provided by the extended Solow model for why some countries are rich and others are poor. Countries are rich because they have high investment rates in physical capital, spend a large fraction of time accumulating skills ($h = e^{\psi u}$), have low population growth rates, and have high levels of technology. Furthermore, in the steady state, per capita output grows at the rate of technological progress, g, just as in the original Solow model.

How well does this model perform empirically in terms of explaining why some countries are richer than others? Because incomes are growing over time, it is useful to analyze the model in terms of *relative* incomes. If we define per capita income relative to the United States to be

$$\hat{y}^* = \frac{y^*}{y_{US}^*},$$

then from equation (3.8), relative incomes are given by

$$\hat{y}^* = \left(\frac{\hat{s}_K}{\hat{x}}\right)^{\alpha/(1-\alpha)} \hat{h}\hat{A}, \tag{3.9}$$

where the "hat" ($\hat{\ }$) is used to denote a variable relative to its U.S. value, and $x \equiv n+g+d$. Notice, however, that unless countries are all growing at the same rate, even relative incomes will not be constant. That is, if the United Kingdom and the United States are growing at different rates, then y_{UK}/y_{US} will not be constant.

In order for relative incomes to be constant in the steady state, we need to make the assumption that g is the same in all countries — that is, the rate of technological progress in all countries is identical. On the surface, this seems very much at odds with one of our key stylized facts from Chapter 1: that growth rates vary substantially across countries. We will discuss technology in much greater detail in later chapters, but for now, notice that if g varies across countries, then the "income gap" between countries eventually becomes infinite. This may not seem plausible if growth is driven purely by technology. Technologies may flow across international borders through international trade, or in scientific journals and newspapers, or through the immigration of scientists and engineers. It may be more plausible to think that technology transfer will keep even the poorest countries from falling too far behind, and one way to interpret this statement is that the growth rates of technology, g, are the same across countries. We will formalize this argument in Chapter 6. In the meantime, notice that in no way are we requiring the *levels* of technology to be the same; in fact, differences in technology presumably explain to a great extent why some countries are richer than others.

Still, we are left wondering why it is that countries have grown at such different rates over the last thirty years if they have the same underlying growth rate for technology. It may seem that the Solow model cannot answer this question, but in fact it provides a very good answer that will be discussed in the next section. First, however, we return to the basic question of how well the extended Solow model fits the data.

By obtaining estimates of the variables and parameters in equation (3.9), we can examine the "fit" of the neoclassical growth model: empirically, how well does it explain why some countries are rich and others are poor?

Figure 3.1 compares the actual levels of GDP per worker in 1990 to the levels predicted by equation (3.9). To use the equation, we assume a physical capital share of $\alpha = 1/3$. This choice fits well with the observation that the share of GDP paid to capital is about 1/3. We measure u as the average educational attainment of the labor force (in years) and assume that $\psi = .10$. Such a value implies that each year of schooling increases a worker's wage by 10 percent, a number roughly consistent

FIGURE 3.1   THE "FIT" OF THE NEOCLASSICAL GROWTH MODEL, 1990

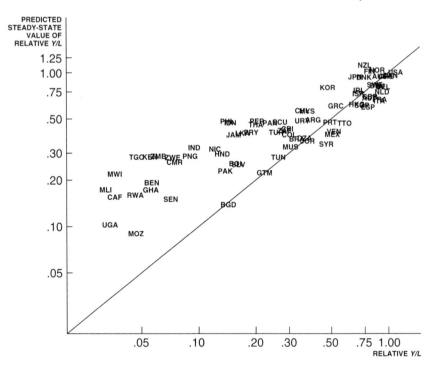

Note: A log scale is used for each axis.

with international evidence on returns to schooling.[5] In addition, we assume that $g + d = .075$ for all countries; we will discuss the assumption that g is the same in all countries in later chapters, and there is no good data on differences in d across countries. Finally, we assume that the technology level, A, is the same across countries. That is, we tie one hand behind our back to see how well the model performs without introducing technological differences. This assumption will be relaxed shortly. The data used in this exercise are listed in Appendix B at the end of the book.

Without accounting for differences in technology, the neoclassical model still describes the distribution of per capita income across countries fairly well. Countries such as the United States and New Zealand are quite rich, as predicted by the model. Countries such as Uganda and Mozambique are decidedly poor. The main failure of the model — that it ignores differences in technology — can be seen by the departures from the 45-degree line in Figure 3.1: the model predicts that the poorest countries should be richer than they are.

How can we incorporate actual technology levels into the calculation? A simple method uses the production function to compute the level of A for each economy. For example, solving equation (3.5) for A yields

$$A = \left(\frac{y}{k}\right)^{\alpha/1-\alpha} \frac{y}{h}.$$

With data on GDP per worker, capital per worker, and educational attainment for each country, we can use this equation to estimate actual levels of A. Incorporating these technology levels (computed for the year 1990) into equation (3.9) improves the fit of the neoclassical model considerably, as shown in Figure 3.2: countries now lie very close to the 45-degree line. The implication is clear. Countries like Uganda and Mozambique are poor because they have low investment rates, low levels of educational attainment, and low levels of technology. Countries like those in the Organization for Economic Cooperation

---

[5] See Jones (1996) for additional details. Notice that measuring u as years of schooling means that it is no longer between zero and one. This problem can be addressed by dividing years of schooling by potential lifespan, which simply changes the value of ψ proportionally and is therefore ignored.

FIGURE 3.2   THE "FIT" INCORPORATING TECHNOLOGICAL DIFFERENCES, 1990

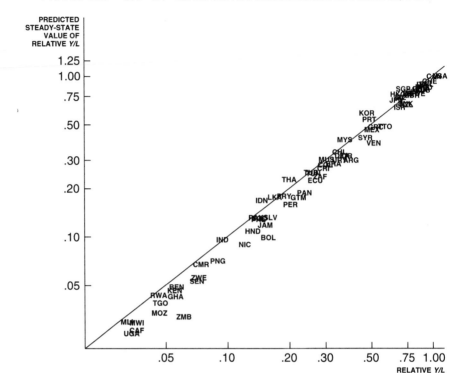

Note: A log scale is used for each axis.

and Development (OECD) are rich because they have high values of these determinants.

A more detailed look at the data and the evidence is provided by Table 3.1. The first two columns of this table report actual and predicted values for GDP per worker relative to the United States. Confirming the results shown in Figure 3.2, the model broadly predicts which countries will be rich and which will be poor. In particular, the model distinguishes well between countries such as the United States, Germany, and France, and countries such as India and Uganda.

A closer look at the estimates of A reported in Table 3.1 reveals an interesting finding: although levels of A are highly correlated with levels of income, the correlation is not perfect. In particular, countries like France and Hong Kong have very high estimates of A. This observation

TABLE 3.1 DATA AND PREDICTIONS FOR THE NEOCLASSICAL MODEL						
	y/y_{US}					
	actual 1990	predicted SS value	s_K	u	n	$\hat{A}_{90}$
U.S.A.	1.00	1.00	0.210	11.8	0.009	1.00
West Germany	0.80	0.83	0.245	8.5	0.003	1.02
Japan	0.61	0.71	0.338	8.5	0.006	0.76
France	0.82	0.85	0.252	6.5	0.005	1.28
U.K.	0.73	0.76	0.171	8.7	0.002	1.10
Argentina	0.36	0.30	0.146	6.7	0.014	0.61
India	0.09	0.10	0.144	3.0	0.021	0.30
Zimbabwe	0.07	0.06	0.131	2.6	0.034	0.20
Uganda	0.03	0.02	0.018	1.9	0.024	0.25
Hong Kong	0.62	0.77	0.195	7.5	0.012	1.25
Taiwan	0.50	0.64	0.237	7.0	0.013	0.99
South Korea	0.43	0.59	0.299	7.8	0.012	0.74

SOURCE: Penn World Tables Mark 5.6, an update of Summers and Heston (1991), and author's calculations.

Note: The investment rates and population growth rates are averages for the period 1980–90. u denotes the average years of schooling of the labor force in 1985. $\hat{A}_{90}$ reports the estimated ratio of A/A_{US} in 1990. The second column of data reports predicted steady-state relative income using this data, as discussed in the text.

leads to an important remark: estimates of A computed this way are like the residuals from growth accounting: they incorporate *any* differences in production not factored in through the inputs. For example, we have not controlled for differences in the quality of educational systems across countries, so that these differences will be included in A. In this sense, it would be more correct to refer to these estimates as total factor productivity levels rather than technology levels.[6]

[6]Hall and Jones (1996) explore these differences more carefully.

The Solow framework is extremely successful in helping us to understand the wide variation in the wealth of nations. Countries that invest
a large fraction of their resources in physical capital and in the accumulation of skills are rich. Countries that use these inputs productively are
rich. The countries that fail in one or more of these dimensions suffer
a corresponding reduction in income. Of course, one thing the Solow
model does not help us understand is *why* some countries invest more
than others, and *why* some countries attain higher levels of technology
or productivity. Addressing these questions is the subject of Chapter 7.
As a preview, the answers are tied intimately to government policies
and institutions.

3.2 CONVERGENCE AND EXPLAINING DIFFERENCES IN GROWTH RATES

We have discussed in detail the ability of the neoclassical model to
explain differences in income levels across economies, but how well
does it perform at explaining differences in growth rates? An early
hypothesis proposed by economic historians such as Aleksander Gerschenkron (1952) and Moses Abramovitz (1986) was that, at least under
certain circumstances, "backward" countries would tend to grow faster
than rich countries, in order to close the gap between the two groups.
This catch-up phenomenon is referred to as *convergence*. For obvious
reasons, questions about convergence have been at the heart of much
empirical work on growth. We documented in Chapter 1 the enormous
differences in levels of income per person around the world: the typical person in the United States earns the annual income of the typical
person in Ethiopia in less than ten days. The question of convergence
asks whether these enormous differences are getting smaller over time.

An important reason why convergence might occur is technology
transfer, but the neoclassical growth model provides another explanation for convergence that we will explore in this section. First, however,
let's examine the empirical evidence on convergence.

William Baumol (1986), alert to the analysis provided by economic
historians, was one of the first economists to provide statistical evidence
documenting convergence among some countries and the absence of
convergence among others. The first piece of evidence presented by
Baumol is displayed in Figure 3.3, which plots per capita GDP (on a

FIGURE 3.3   **PER CAPITA GDP, 1870—1994**

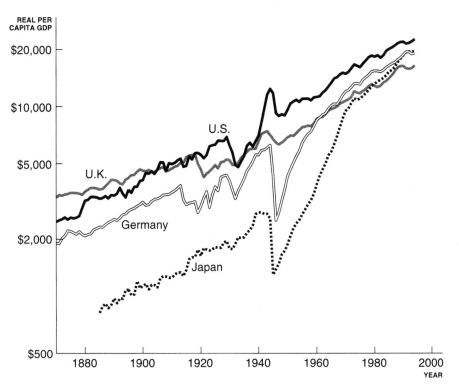

log scale) for several industrialized economies from 1870 to 1994. The narrowing of the gaps between countries is evident in this figure. Interestingly, the "leader" in terms of per capita GDP in 1870 was Australia (not shown). The United Kingdom had the second-highest per capita GDP and was recognized as the industrial center of the Western world. Around the turn of the century, the United States surpassed Australia and the United Kingdom and has remained the "leader" ever since.

Figure 3.4 reveals the ability of the convergence hypothesis to explain why some countries grew fast and others grew slowly over the course of the last century. The graph plots a country's initial per capita GDP (in 1885) against the country's growth rate from 1885 to 1994. The figure reveals a strong negative relationship between the two variables: countries such as Australia and the United Kingdom, which were relatively rich in 1885, grew most slowly, while countries like Japan that

FIGURE 3.4   GROWTH RATE VERSUS INITIAL PER CAPITA GDP, 1885–1994

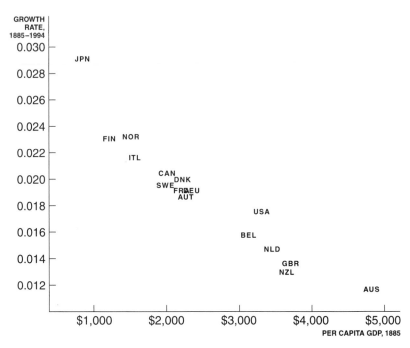

were relatively poor grew most rapidly. The simple convergence hypothesis seems to do a good job of explaining differences in growth rates, at least among this sample of industrialized economies.[7]

Figures 3.5 and 3.6 plot growth rates versus initial GDP per capita for the OECD and the world for the period 1960–90. Figure 3.5 shows that the convergence hypothesis works extremely well for explaining growth rates across the OECD for the period examined. But before we declare the hypothesis a success, note that Figure 3.6 shows that the convergence hypothesis fails to explain differences in growth rates across the world as a whole. Baumol also reported this finding: across large samples of countries, it does not appear that poor countries grow faster than rich countries. The poor countries are not "closing the gap" that

[7]J. Bradford De Long (1988) provides an important criticism of this result. See Exercise 4 at the end of this chapter.

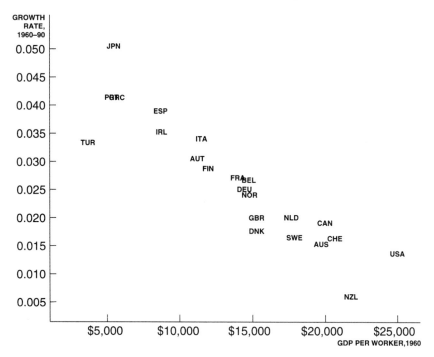

FIGURE 3.5   CONVERGENCE IN THE OECD, 1960-90

exists in per capita incomes. (Recall that Table 1.1 in Chapter 1 supports this finding.)

Why, then, do we see convergence among some sets of countries but a lack of convergence among the countries of the world as a whole? The neoclassical growth model suggests an important explanation for these findings.

Consider the key differential equation of the neoclassical growth model, given in equation (3.7). This equation can be rewritten as

$$\frac{\dot{\tilde{k}}}{\tilde{k}} = s_K \frac{\tilde{y}}{\tilde{k}} - (n + g + d). \tag{3.10}$$

Remember that $\tilde{y}$ is equal to $\tilde{k}^{\alpha}$. Therefore, the average product of capital $\tilde{y}/\tilde{k}$ is equal to $\tilde{k}^{\alpha-1}$. In particular, it declines as $\tilde{k}$ rises, because of the diminishing returns to capital accumulation in the neoclassical model.

FIGURE 3.6   THE LACK OF CONVERGENCE FOR THE WORLD, 1960–90

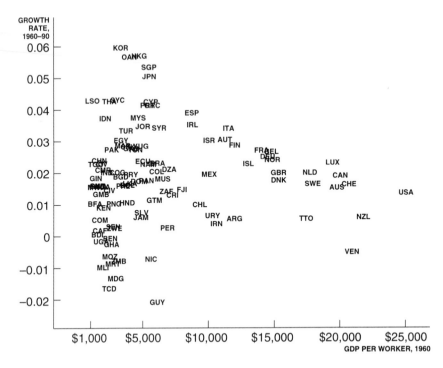

As in Chapter 2, we can analyze this equation in a simple diagram, shown in Figure 3.7. The two curves in the figure plot the two terms on the right-hand side of equation (3.10). Therefore, the difference between the curves is the growth rate of $\tilde{k}$. Notice that the growth rate of $\tilde{y}$ is simply proportional to this difference. Furthermore, because the growth rate of technology is constant, any changes in the growth rates of $\tilde{k}$ and $\tilde{y}$ must be due to changes in the growth rates of capital per worker, k, and output per worker, y.

Suppose the economy of InitiallyBehind starts with the capital-technology ratio $\tilde{k}_{IB}$ shown on Figure 3.7, while the neighboring economy of InitiallyAhead starts with the higher capital-technology ratio indicated by $\tilde{k}_{IA}$. If these two economies have the same levels of technology, the same rates of investment, and the same rates of population growth, then InitiallyBehind will temporarily grow faster than InitiallyAhead. The output-per-worker gap between the two countries

FIGURE 3.7   TRANSITION DYNAMICS IN THE NEOCLASSICAL MODEL

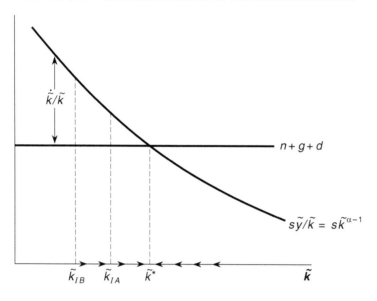

will narrow over time as both economies approach the same steady state. An important prediction of the neoclassical model is this: *Among countries that have the same steady state, the convergence hypothesis should hold: poor countries should grow faster on average than rich countries.*

For members of the OECD or the industrialized countries, the assumption that their economies have similar technology levels, investment rates, and population growth rates may not be a bad one. The neoclassical model, then, would predict the convergence that we saw in Figures 3.4 and 3.5. This same reasoning suggests a compelling explanation for the *lack* of convergence across the world as a whole: all countries do not have the same steady states. In fact, as we saw in Figure 3.2, the differences in income levels around the world largely reflect differences in steady states. Because all countries do not have the same investment rates, population growth rates, or technology levels, they are not generally expected to grow toward the same steady-state target.

Another important prediction of the neoclassical model is related to growth rates. This prediction, which can be found in many growth models, is important enough that we will give it a name, the "principle of transition dynamics":

The further an economy is "below" its steady state, the faster the economy should grow. The further an economy is "above" its steady state, the slower the economy should grow.[8]

This principle is clearly illustrated by the analysis of equation (3.10) provided in Figure 3.7. Although it is a key feature of the neoclassical model, the principle of transition dynamics applies much more broadly. In Chapters 5 and 6, for example, we will see that it is also a feature of the models of new growth theory that endogenize technological progress.

Mankiw et al. (1992) and Barro and Sala-i-Martin (1992) show that this prediction of the neoclassical model can explain differences in growth rates across the countries of the world. Figure 3.8 illustrates this point by plotting the growth rate of GDP per worker from 1960 to 1990 against the deviation (in logs) of GDP per worker in 1960 from the steady-state values, predicted as in Table 3.1. Comparing Figure 3.6 and Figure 3.8, one sees that although poorer countries do not necessarily grow faster, countries that are "poor" relative to their own steady states do tend to grow more rapidly. In 1960, good examples of these countries were Korea, Japan, Singapore, and Hong Kong — economies that grew rapidly over the next 30 years, just as the neoclassical model would predict.[9]

This analysis of convergence has been extended by a number of authors to different sets of economies. For example, Barro and Sala-i-Martin (1991, 1992) show that the U.S. states, regions of France, and prefectures in Japan all exhibit "unconditional" convergence similar

---

[8]In simple models, including most of those presented in this book, this principle works well. In more complicated models with more state variables, however, it must be modified.

[9]Mankiw, Romer and Weil (1992) and Barro and Sala-i-Martin (1992) have called this phenomenon "conditional convergence," because it reflects the convergence of countries after we control for ("condition on") differences in steady states. It is important to keep in mind what this "conditional convergence" result means. It is simply a confirmation of a result predicted by the neoclassical growth model: that countries with similar steady states will exhibit convergence. It does not mean that all countries in the world are converging to the same steady state, only that they are converging to their own steady states according to a common theoretical model.

FIGURE 3.8   "CONDITIONAL" CONVERGENCE FOR THE WORLD, 1960—90

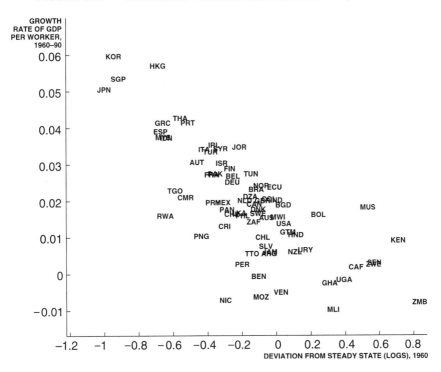

Note: The U.S. deviation (in logs) from steady state in 1960 is normalized to zero. Estimates of A for 1970 instead of 1990 are used to compute the steady state.

to what we've observed in the OECD. This matches the prediction of the Solow model if regions within a country are similar in terms of investment and population growth, as seems reasonable.

How does the neoclassical model account for the wide differences in growth rates across countries documented in Chapter 1? The principle of transition dynamics provides the answer: countries that have not reached their steady states are not expected to grow at the same rate. Those "below" their steady states will grow rapidly, and those "above" their steady states will grow slowly.

As we saw in Chapter 2, there are many reasons why countries may not be in steady state. An increase in the investment rate, a change in the population growth rate, or an event like World War II that destroys much of a country's capital stock will generate a gap between current income and steady-state income. This gap will change growth rates until the economy returns to its steady-state path. Other "shocks" can also cause temporary differences in growth rates. For example, large changes in oil prices will have important effects on the economic performance of oil-exporting countries. Mismanagement of the macro economy can similarly generate temporary changes in growth performance. The hyperinflations in many Latin American countries during the 1980s are a good example of this. Working in the other direction, policy reforms that shift the steady-state path of an economy upward can generate increases in growth rates along a transition path. Increases in the investment rate, skill accumulation, or the level of technology will have this effect.[10]

3.3 THE EVOLUTION OF THE INCOME DISTRIBUTION

Convergence, the closing of the gap between rich and poor economies, is just one possible outcome among many that could be occuring. Alternatively, perhaps the poorest countries are falling behind while countries with "intermediate" incomes are converging toward the rich. Or perhaps countries are not getting any closer together at all but are instead fanning out, with the rich countries getting richer and the poor countries getting poorer. More generally, these questions are really about the evolution of the distribution of per capita incomes around the world.[11]

Figure 3.9 illustrates a key fact about the evolution of the income distribution: for the world as a whole, the enormous gaps in income across countries have generally not narrowed over time. This figure plots the ratio of GDP per worker in the 5th-richest country to GDP per worker in the 5th-poorest country. In 1960, GDP per worker of the fifth-richest country was more than 25 times that of the fifth-poorest country. If anything, the gap was even higher in 1990.

While Figure 3.9 shows that the "width" of the income distribution has not declined, Figure 3.10 examines changes at each point in the

---

[10]Barro (1991) and Easterly, Kremer, et al. (1993) provide empirical analyses of why countries have exhibited different growth rates since 1960.

[11]Jones (1997a) provides an overview of the literature on the world income distribution. Quah (1993, 1996) discusses this topic in more detail.

FIGURE 3.9   INCOME RATIOS, 5TH-RICHEST COUNTRY TO 5TH-POOREST COUNTRY, 1960—90

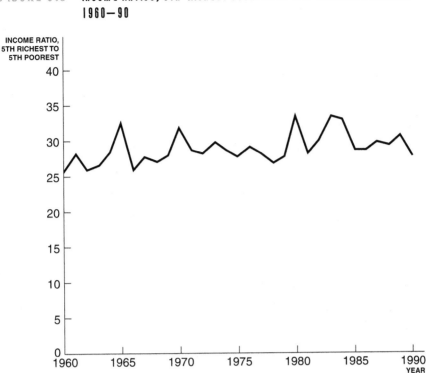

income distribution. According to the figure, 50 percent of the countries had relative incomes that were less than 20 percent of U.S. GDP per worker in 1960; 80 percent of the countries had relative incomes less than 40 percent of U.S. GDP per worker. By 1990, these numbers had improved, particularly at the upper end: the 50th percentile was slightly more than 20 percent of U.S. GDP per worker while the 80th percentile was more than 60 percent. In contrast, the poorest economies — those below the 30th percentile, for example — actually had relative incomes in 1990 lower than in 1960. In this sense, one might say there was some "catch-up" or "convergence" at the middle and top of the income distribution from 1960 to 1990, but "divergence" at the bottom end.[12]

[12]It is interesting to compare this figure to the results in Chapter 1. An important difference is that the unit of observation here is the *country*; the unit of observation for the distributions computed in Chapter 1 was the *individual*.

FIGURE 3.10   **THE EVOLUTION OF THE WORLD INCOME DISTRIBUTION, 1960 AND 1990**

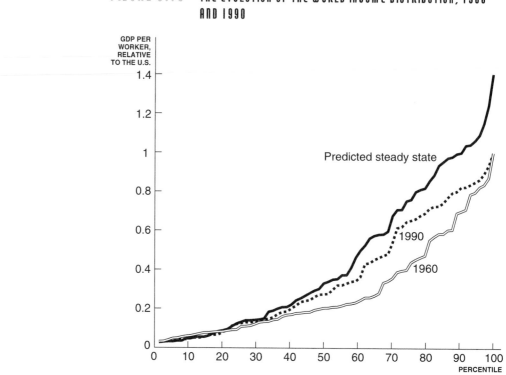

Note: A point (x, y) in the figure indicates that x percent of countries had relative GDP per worker less than or equal to y. Seventy-four countries are represented.

The neoclassical model allows us to consider how the income distribution is likely to evolve in the future. Recall that Figure 3.2 examined relative incomes in 1990 compared to the steady-state relative incomes predicted by the neoclassical model. Although the fit of the neoclassical model was good, it was not perfect, and one way of interpreting this is that the income distribution is still evolving. In addition, rates of investment in human capital are rising for a number of countries, providing further reason for the income distribution to evolve.

The third line in Figure 3.10 plots a simple forecast of the distribution of steady-state relative income levels.[13] Some interesting results are

[13]The only difference relative to the steady states reported in Table 3.1 is that current enrollment rates are used to forecast the future educational attainment of the labor force in each country. See Jones (1996) for details.

evident. First, at the top of the income distribution, a number of economies are predicted to have relative incomes that *exceed* that of the
United States. These economies include Singapore, France, Spain, and
Italy. Why does this occur? The answer is straightforward: in the neoclassical model, relative incomes are determined by investment rates
and population growth rates, and the U.S. investment rates are not the
highest in the world. As of 1990, the U.S. productivity level and educational attainment compensate for this, but assuming the distribution
of productivity levels remains the same over time, this lead cannot persist according to the model. Moreover, to the extent that countries like
Japan experience an increase in their relative productivity levels, as
seems reasonable, the relative position of the United States could be
even lower in the long run.

How seriously should we take this prediction? The relatively low
rates of investment undertaken in the United States have been a source
of concern to economists for a number of years. In many ways, the prediction concerning the evolution of the income distribution is simply
a natural result of this fact. As just mentioned, whatever technological
lead the United States has is likely to get smaller, reinforcing this general
trend at the top of the income distribution. Moreover, there is historical
precedent for such a change: at the turn of the century, Australia and the
United Kingdom were at the top of the income distribution, and before
that the Netherlands probably had the highest per capita income. At
the same time, however, the extremely high investment rates observed
in countries such as Singapore and Japan are unlikely to persist over
time, perhaps allowing the United States to maintain its high relative
income.

Another interesting prediction about the shape of the income distribution concerns the economies at the bottom of the distribution. As
shown in Figure 3.10, there is no tendency for the relative incomes of the
low-income countries to increase according to the neoclassical model.
Instead, for these countries, the low incomes appear to be steady-state
outcomes. This is also seen by the relatively good fit of the model at low
incomes in Figure 3.2. If anything, these countries appear to exhibit a
decline in relative income. Overall, then, we see that it is difficult to
characterize the near-term evolution of the world income distribution
with a single word like "convergence" or "divergence." At the bottom,
the low-income countries are predicted either to stay the same relative
to the United States, or perhaps even to see a decline in relative income.

On the other hand, at the top of the income distribution, several countries are predicted to continue catching up to the United States, and it
seems likely that some could surpass U.S. per capita income.[14]

EXERCISES

1. *Where are these economies headed?* Consider the following data:

	$\hat{y}_{90}$	s_K	u	n	$\hat{A}_{90}$
U.S.A.	1.00	0.210	11.8	0.009	1.00
Canada	0.93	0.253	10.4	0.010	1.05
Brazil	0.30	0.169	3.7	0.021	0.77
China	0.06	0.222	7.6	0.014	0.11
Kenya	0.05	0.126	4.5	0.037	0.16

   Assume that $g + d = .075$, $\alpha = 1/3$, and $\phi = .10$ for all countries. Using analysis like that reported in Table 3.1, estimate the steady-state
   incomes of these economies, relative to the United States. Consider
   two extreme cases: (a) the 1990 TFP ratios are maintained, and (b)
   the TFP levels converge completely. For each case, which economy
   will grow fastest in the next decade and which slowest? Why?

2. *What are state variables?* The basic idea of solving dynamic models
   that contain a differential equation is to first write the model so that
   along a balanced growth path, some state variable is constant. In
   Chapter 2, we used y/A and k/A as state variables. In this chapter,
   we used y/Ah and k/Ah. Recall, however, that h is a constant. This
   reasoning suggests that one should be able to solve the model using
   y/A and k/A as the state variables. Do this. That is, solve the growth
   model in equations (3.1) to (3.4) to get the solution in equation (3.8)
   using y/A and k/A as state variables.

---

[14]Lant Pritchett (1997) makes the interesting observation that divergence characterizes
the world income distribution over the very long run. A million years ago, for example, we
were all hunters and gatherers with subsistence income. Today, some economies remain
very close to the subsistence level, while others are substantially richer.

3. *Galton's fallacy* (based on Quah, 1993). During the late 1800s, Sir Francis Galton, a famous statistician in England, studied the distribution of heights in the British population and how the distribution was evolving over time. In particular, Galton noticed that the sons of tall fathers tended to be shorter than their fathers, and vice versa. Galton worried that this implied some kind of regression toward "mediocrity."

   Suppose that we have a population of 10 mothers who have 10 daughters. Suppose that their heights are determined as follows. Place 10 sheets of paper in a hat labeled with heights of $5'1''$, $5'2''$, $5'3''$, ... $5'10''$. Draw a number from the hat and let that be the height for a mother. Without replacing the sheet just drawn, continue. Now suppose that the heights of the daughters are determined in the same way, starting with the hat full again and drawing new heights. Will tall mothers tend to have shorter daughters, and vice versa?

   Let the heights correspond to income levels, and consider observing income levels at two points in time, say 1960 and 1990. What does Galton's fallacy imply about a plot of growth rates against initial income? Does this mean the figures in this chapter are useless?[15]

4. *Reconsidering the Baumol results.* J. Bradford De Long (1988), in a comment on Baumol's convergence result for the industrialized countries over the last century, pointed out that the result could be driven by the procedure through which the countries were selected. In particular, De Long noted two things. First, only countries that were rich at the end of the sample (i.e., in the 1980s) were included. Second, several countries not included, such as Argentina, were richer than Japan in 1870. Use these points to criticize and discuss the Baumol results. Do these criticisms apply to the results for the OECD? For the world?

5. *The Mankiw-Romer-Weil (1992) model.* As mentioned in this chapter, the extended Solow model that we have considered differs slightly from that in Mankiw, Romer and Weil (1992). This problem asks you to solve their model. The key difference is the treatment of human capital. Mankiw, Romer and Weil assume that human capital

---

[15] See Quah (1993) and Friedman (1992).

is accumulated just like physical capital, so that it is measured in units of output instead of years of time.

Assume production is given by $Y = K^\alpha H^\beta (AL)^{1-\alpha-\beta}$, where α and β are constants between zero and one whose sum is also between zero and one. Human capital is accumulated just like physical capital:

$$\dot{H} = s_H Y - dH,$$

where s_H is the constant share of output invested in human capital. Assume that physical capital is accumulated as in equation (3.4), that the labor force grows at rate n, and that technological progress occurs at rate g. Solve the model for the path of output per worker $y \equiv Y/L$ along the balanced growth path as a function of s_K, s_H, n, g, d, α, and β. Discuss how the solution differs from that in equation (3.8). *Hint:* Define state variables such as y/A, h/A, and k/A.

4 THE ECONOMICS OF IDEAS

T he neoclassical models we have studied so far are in many ways capital-based theories of economic growth. These theories focus on modeling the accumulation of physical and human capital. In another sense, however, the theories emphasize the importance of technology. For example, the models do not generate economic growth in the absence of technological progress, and productivity differences help to explain why some countries are rich and others are poor. In this way, neoclassical growth theory highlights its own shortcoming: although technology is a central component of neoclassical theory, it is left unmodeled. Technological improvements arrive exogenously at a constant rate, g, and differences in technologies across economies are unexplained. In this chapter, we will explore the broad issues associated with creating an economic model of technology and technological improvement.

4.1 WHAT IS TECHNOLOGY?

In the economics of growth and development, the term technology has a very specific meaning: *technology* is the way inputs to the production process are transformed into output. For example, if we have a general production function $Y = F(K, L, \cdot)$, then the technology of production is given by the function $F(\cdot)$; this production function explains how inputs are transformed into output. In the Cobb-Douglas production function of earlier chapters, $Y = K^{\alpha}(AL)^{1-\alpha}$, A is an index of technology.[1]

Ideas improve the technology of production. A new idea allows a given bundle of inputs to produce more or better output. A good example of an idea was provided by Paul Romer (1990). Neanderthals used iron oxide as a pigment to create drawings on the walls of caves. Now, we "paint" iron oxide onto magnetic tape to produce VCR recordings. The "idea" behind the VCR allows us to use a given bundle of inputs to produce output that generates a higher level of utility. In the context of the production function above, a new idea generates an increase in the technology index, A.

Examples of ideas and technological improvements abound. Moore's Law (attributed to the chairman of Intel, Gordon Moore) asserts that the number of transistors that can be packed onto a computer chip doubles approximately every 18 months. In 1800, light was provided by candles and oil lamps, whereas today we have very efficient fluorescent bulbs. William Nordhaus (1994) has calculated that the quality-adjusted price of light has fallen by a factor of 4,000 since the year 1800.[2]

Ideas are by no means limited to feats of engineering, however. Sam Walton's creation of the Wal-Mart approach to retailing is no less an idea than advances in semiconductor technology. The multiplex theater and diet soft drinks are innovations that allowed firms to combine inputs in new ways that consumers, according to revealed preference, have found very valuable. The assembly lines and mass production techniques that allowed Henry Ford's company to turn out a Model T every 24 seconds, and Ford's payment of $5-day wages when the prevailing wage was less than half that amount are business innovations that profoundly changed U.S. manufacturing.

---

[1] The parameter α is also part of the "technology" of production.
[2] See the *Economist*, October 22, 1994, p. 84.

4.2 THE ECONOMICS OF IDEAS

Beginning in the mid-1980s, Paul Romer formalized the relationship between the economics of ideas and economic growth.[3] This relationship can be thought of in the following way:

$$\text{Ideas} \longrightarrow \text{Nonrivalry} \longrightarrow \begin{array}{c}\text{Increasing}\\\text{Returns}\end{array} \longrightarrow \begin{array}{c}\text{Imperfect}\\\text{Competition}\end{array}$$

According to Romer, an inherent characteristic of ideas is that they are nonrivalrous. This nonrivalry implies the presence of increasing returns to scale. And to model these increasing returns in a competitive environment with intentional research necessarily requires imperfect competition. Each of these terms and the links between them will now be discussed in detail. In the next chapter, we will develop the mathematical model that integrates this reasoning.

A crucial observation emphasized by Romer (1990) is that ideas are very different from most other economic goods. Most goods, such as compact-disc (CD) players or lawyer services are *rivalrous*. That is, my use of a CD player excludes your use of the same CD player, or my seeing a particular attorney today from 1:00 P.M. to 2:00 P.M. precludes your seeing the same attorney at the same time. Most economic goods share this property: the use of the good by one person precludes its use by another. If one thousand people each want to use a CD player, we have to provide them with one thousand CD players.

In contrast, ideas are *nonrivalrous*. The fact that Toyota takes advantage of just-in-time inventory methods does not preclude GM from taking advantage of the same technique. Once an idea has been created, anyone with knowledge of the idea can take advantage of it. Consider the design for the next-generation computer chip. Once the design itself has been created, factories throughout the country and even the world can use the design simultaneously to produce computer chips, provided they have the plans in hand. The paper the plans are written on is rivalrous; the skills needed to understand the plans are rivalrous; but the instructions written on the paper — the ideas — are not.

---

[3] This basic insight is found in Phelps (1966), Shell (1967), and Romer (1986).

This last observation suggests another important characteristic of ideas, one that ideas share with most economic goods: they are, at least partially, *excludable*. The degree to which a good is excludable is the degree to which the owner of the good can charge a fee for its use. The firm that invents the design for the next computer chip can presumably lock the plans in a safe and restrict access to the design, at least for some period of time. Alternatively, copyright and patent systems grant inventors who receive copyrights or patents the right to charge for the use of their ideas.

Figure 4.1, taken in large part from Romer (1993), lists a variety of economic goods according to their degree of excludability and whether they are rivalrous or nonrivalrous. Both rivalrous and nonrivalrous goods vary in the degree to which they are excludable. Goods such as a CD player, a floppy disk, or the services of a lawyer are highly excludable.

FIGURE 4.1   ECONOMIC ATTRIBUTES OF SELECTED GOODS

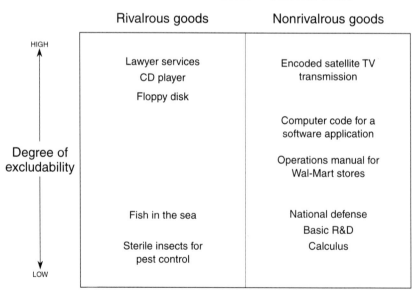

SOURCE: This is a slightly altered version of Figure 1 in Romer (1993).

Goods that suffer from the "tragedy of the commons" problem are rivalrous but have a low degree of excludability.[4] The classic example of such goods is the overgrazing of common land shared by English peasants during the Middle Ages. The cost of one peasant choosing to graze an additional cow on the commons is shared by all of the peasants, but the benefit is captured solely by one peasant. The result is an inefficiently high level of grazing that can potentially destroy the commons. A similar outcome occurs when a group of friends goes to a nice restaurant and divides the bill evenly at the end of the evening — suddenly everyone wants to order an expensive bottle of wine and a rich chocolate dessert. A modern example of the commons problem is the overfishing of international waters.

Ideas are nonrivalrous goods, but they vary substantially in their degree of excludability. Encoded satellite TV transmissions are highly excludable, while computer software is less excludable. Both of these goods or ideas are essentially a collection of 1's and 0's ordered in a particular way so as to convey information. The digital signals of an encoded satellite transmission are scrambled so as to be useful only to someone with a decoder. In contrast, computer software is often "unscrambled": anyone with a disk drive can copy software to give to a friend. Software companies take advantage of this aspect of ideas in manufacturing software but can also find it to be a problem because of software pirating. Similar considerations apply to the operating manual for Wal-Mart. Sam Walton details his ideas for efficiently running a retail operation in the manual and gives it to all of his stores. However, some of these ideas may be copied by an astute observer of Wal-Mart's business behavior.

Nonrivalrous goods that are essentially unexcludable are often called *public goods*. A traditional example is national defense. For example, consider the often-debated "Star Wars" defense shield that would protect the United States from hostile missiles. If the shield is going to protect *some* citizens in Washington, D.C., it will protect *all* citizens in the nation's capital; the "Star Wars" defense system is nonrivalrous and unexcludable. Some ideas may also be both nonrivalrous and unexcludable. For example, the results of basic research and development (R&D) may by their very nature be unexcludable. Calculus, our scientific

[4]See Hardin (1968).

understanding of medicine, and the Black-Scholes formula for pricing financial options are other examples.[5]

The economics of goods depends on their attributes. Goods that are excludable allow their producers to capture the benefits they produce; goods that are not excludable involve substantial "spillovers" of benefits that are not captured by producers. Such spillovers are called *externalities.* Goods with positive spillovers tend to be underproduced by markets, providing a classic opportunity for government intervention to improve welfare. For example, basic R&D and national defense are financed primarily by the government. Goods with negative spillovers may be overproduced by markets, and government regulation may be needed if property rights cannot be well defined. The tragedy of the commons is a good example.

Goods that are rivalrous must be produced each time they are sold; goods that are nonrivalrous need to be produced only once. That is, nonrivalrous goods such as ideas involve a fixed cost of production and zero marginal cost. For example, it costs a great deal to produce the first unit of the latest word processor or spreadsheet, but subsequent units are produced simply by copying the software from the first unit. It required a great deal of inspiration and perspiration for Thomas Edison and his lab to produce the first commercially viable electric light. But once the first light was produced, additional lights could be produced at a much lower per-unit cost. In both the spreadsheet and the lightbulb examples, notice that the only reason for a nonzero marginal cost is that the nonrivalrous good — the idea — is embodied in a rivalrous good — the floppy disk or the materials of the lightbulb.

This reasoning leads to a simple but powerful insight: the economics of "ideas" is intimately tied to the presence of increasing returns to scale and imperfect competition. The link to increasing returns is almost immediate once we grant that ideas are associated with fixed costs. Returning to the software example, the "idea" underlying the next generation of word processing (perhaps with voice recognition, let's say) requires a one-time research cost. Once the product is developed, each additional unit is produced with constant returns to scale: doubling the number of

---

[5]Fischer Black and Myron Scholes (1972) developed an elegant mathematical technique for pricing a financial security called an option. The formula is widely used on Wall Street and throughout the financial community.

floppy disks, instruction manuals, and labor to put everything together will double production. In other words, this process can be viewed as production with a fixed cost and a constant marginal cost.

Figure 4.2 plots a production function $y = f(x) = 100 * (x - F)$ that exhibits a fixed cost F and a constant marginal cost of production. Think of y as copies of the next generation of word-processing software with voice recognition (let's call it "WordTalk"), and think of x as the amount of labor input required to produce WordTalk. In this example, F units of labor are required to produce the first copy of WordTalk.[6] Thus, F is the research cost, which is likely to be a very large number. If x is measured as hours of labor input, we might assume that $F = 10,000$: it takes 10,000 hours to produce the first copy of WordTalk. After the first copy is created, additional copies can be produced very cheaply. In our example, one hour of labor input can produce 100 copies of the software.

Recall that a production function exhibits increasing returns to scale if $f(ax) > af(x)$ where a is some number greater than one — for example, doubling the inputs more than doubles output. Clearly, this is the case

FIGURE 4.2   FIXED COSTS AND INCREASING RETURNS

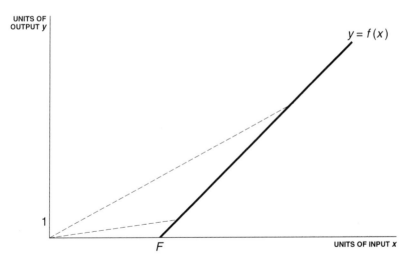

[6]The careful reader will notice that this statement is only approximately right. Actually, $F + 1/100$ units of labor are required to produce the first copy.

for the production function in Figure 4.2. F units of input are required before any output can be produced; $2F$ units of input will produce $100 * F$ units of output. The increasing returns can also be seen in that labor productivity, y/x, is rising with the scale of production.

A common question about software pricing (and the pricing of lots of other goods including CDs, books, and pharmaceuticals) is "If the marginal cost of production is very small, why is it that the product costs so much? Doesn't this imply an inefficiency in the market?" The answer is that yes, there is an inefficiency — remember from your first microeconomics class that efficiency requires that price be equal to marginal cost. However, the inefficiency is in many ways a necessary one.

To see why, Figure 4.3 shows that the presence of a fixed cost, or more generally the presence of increasing returns, implies that setting price equal to marginal cost will result in negative profits. This figure shows the costs of production as a function of the number of units produced. The marginal cost of production is constant — e.g., it costs $10 to produce each additional unit of software. But the average cost is declining. The first unit costs F to produce because of the fixed cost of the idea, which is also the average cost of the first unit. At higher levels

FIGURE 4.3   FIXED COSTS AND INCREASING RETURNS

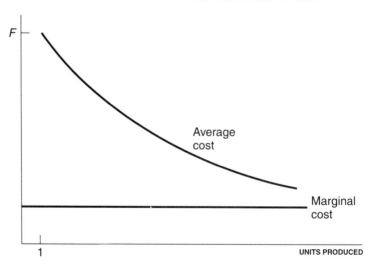

of production, this fixed cost is spread over more and more units so that the average cost declines with scale.

Now consider what happens if this firm sets price equal to marginal cost. *With increasing returns to scale, average cost is always greater than marginal cost and therefore marginal cost pricing results in negative profits.* In other words, no firm would enter this market and pay the fixed cost F to develop the computer software if it could not set the price above the marginal cost of producing additional units. In practice, of course, this is exactly what we see: software sells for tens or hundreds of dollars, when the marginal cost of production is presumably only five or ten dollars. Firms will enter only if they can charge a price higher than marginal cost that allows them to recoup the fixed cost of creating the good in the first place. The production of new goods, or new ideas, requires the possibility of earning profits and therefore necessitates a move away from perfect competition.

4.3 INTELLECTUAL PROPERTY RIGHTS AND THE INDUSTRIAL REVOLUTION

In this chapter, we've explained several key features of the economics of ideas. Central among these features is that the economics of ideas involves potentially large one-time costs to create inventions. Think of the cost of creating the first copy of Windows 95 or the first jet engine. Inventors will not incur these one-time costs unless they have some expectation of being able to capture some of the gains to society, in the form of profit, after they create the invention. Patents and copyrights are legal mechanisms that grant inventors monopoly power for a time in order to allow them to reap a return from their inventions. They are attempts to use the legal system to influence the degree of excludability of ideas. Without the patent or copyright, it may be quite easy for someone to "reverse engineer" an invention and the competition from this imitation might eliminate the incentive for the inventor to create the idea in the first place. According to some economic historians such as 1993 Nobel laureate Douglass C. North, this reasoning is quite important in understanding the broad history of economic growth, as we will now explain.

One of the important facts about world economic growth is that it is a very recent phenomenon. Prior to the Industrial Revolution in Britain, the beginning of which historians date to the 1760s, sustained, rapid growth in per capita income was virtually unknown in the world. The general problem with illustrating this point is that we do not have good data on GDP going back much before 1700 or 1800. However, we can exploit the arguments of Thomas Malthus and use population growth to proxy for income growth.[7] That is, for large spans of history, we conjecture that population and income are closely related. For example, the discovery of a new technique in agriculture initially leads to a temporary increase in income, a reduction in mortality, and therefore to an increase in the rate of population growth as more people can be supported by the available land. Gradually, however, diminishing returns to agriculture lead income to fall back to its original (subsistence) level, albeit with a larger population. It is only when sustained increases in per capita income occur that high, sustained rates of population growth are possible.

With this in mind, consider Figure 4.4, which plots average annual rates of world population growth for the last 2,000 years. For most of the history of the world, population growth was extremely slow. Indeed, Michael Kremer (1993) reports that the average population growth rate from 1 million B.C. to 1 A.D. was 0.0007 percent per year.[8] From 1 A.D. to 1700, the average annual rate of population growth was still only 0.075 percent per year. During the eighteenth century, population growth rates accelerated, and in the last forty years, world population has grown at an average annual rate of nearly 2 percent per year.

To help to place these numbers in perspective, suppose we were to map out world history on a football field. Let the goal line on one end of the field stand for 1 million B.C., which is a conservative estimate of when humans first became distinguishable from other primates. Let the other goal line correspond to 2000 A.D. Humans were essentially hunters and gatherers for the overwhelming majority of history, until the development of agriculture approximately 10,000 years ago. On our football field, hunting and gathering occupies the first 99 yards of the 100-yard field; systematic agriculture begins on the one-yard line. The

---

[7] Kremer (1993) provides a detailed application of this technique.

[8] This example illustrates the remarkable power of compounding: even at this near-zero growth rate, world population increased more than a thousand-fold over this million year period.

FIGURE 4.4   WORLD POPULATION GROWTH, 1 A.D. TO 1990

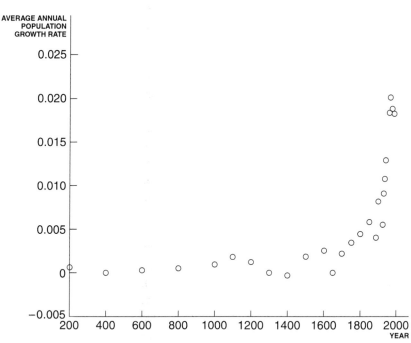

SOURCE: Author's calculations and Kremer (1993).

year 1 A.D. is only 7 inches from the final goal line, and the Industrial Revolution begins less than one inch from the goal line. In the history of humankind, the era of modern economic growth is the width of a golf ball perched at the end of a football field.

Clearly, sustained economic growth is a very recent phenomenon, and this raises one of the fundamental questions of economic history. How did sustained growth get started in the first place? The thesis of Douglass North and a number of other economic historians is that the development of intellectual property rights, a cumulative process that occurred over centuries, is responsible for modern economic growth. It is not until individuals are encouraged by the credible promise of large returns via the marketplace that sustained innovation occurs. To quote a concise statement of this thesis,

What determines the rate of development of new technology and of pure scientific knowledge? In the case of technological change, the social rate of return from developing new techniques had probably always been high; but we would expect that until the means to raise the private rate of return on developing new techniques was devised, there would be slow progress in producing new techniques.... [T]hroughout man's past he has continually developed new techniques, but the pace has been slow and intermittent. The primary reason has been that the incentives for developing new techniques have occurred only sporadically. Typically, innovations could be copied at no cost by others and without any reward to the inventor or innovator. The failure to develop systematic property rights in innovation up until fairly modern times was a major source of the slow pace of technological change (North 1981, p. 164).

A fascinating and illustrative example of this thesis is provided by the history of navigation. Perhaps the foremost obstacle to the development of ocean shipping, international trade, and world exploration was the problem of determining a ship's location at sea. Latitude was easily discerned by the angle of the north star above the horizon. However, determining a ship's longitude at sea — its location in the east–west dimension — was a tremendously important problem that remained unsolved for several centuries. When Columbus landed in the Americas, he thought he had discovered a new route to India because he had no idea of his longitude.

Several astronomical observatories built in western Europe during the seventeenth and eighteenth centuries were sponsored by governments for the express purpose of solving the problem of longitude. The rulers of Spain, Holland, and Britain offered large monetary prizes for the solution. Finally, the problem was solved in the mid-1700s, on the eve of the Industrial Revolution, by a poorly educated but eminently skilled clockmaker in England named John Harrison. Harrison spent his lifetime building and perfecting a mechanical clock, the chronometer, whose accuracy could be maintained despite turbulence and frequent changes in weather over the course of an ocean voyage that might last for months. This chronometer, rather than any astronomical observation, provided the first practical solution to the determination of longitude.

How does a chronometer solve the problem? Imagine taking two wristwatches with you on a cruise from London to New York. Maintain London (Greenwich!) time on one watch, and set the other watch to noon every day when the sun is directly overhead. The difference in times between the two watches reveals one's longitude relative to the prime meridian.[9]

The lesson of this story for the economist is less in the details of how a chronometer solved the problem of longitude and more in the details of what financial incentives led to the solution. From this standpoint, the astounding fact is that there was no *market* mechanism generating the enormous investments required to find a solution. It is not that Harrison or anyone else would become rich from selling the solution to the navies and merchants of western Europe, despite the fact that the benefits to the world from the solution were enormous. Instead, the main financial incentive seems to have been the prizes offered by the governments. Although the Statute of Monopolies in 1624 established a patent law in Britain and the institutions to secure property rights were well on their way in the late eighteenth century, they were still not sufficiently developed to provide the financial incentives for private investment in solving the problem of longitude.[10]

The Industrial Revolution — the beginning of sustained economic growth — occurred when the institutions protecting intellectual property rights were sufficiently well developed that entrepreneurs could capture as a private return some of the enormous social returns their innovations would create. While government incentives such as prizes or public funding could substitute for these market incentives in certain cases (as they ultimately did in the case of the chronometer), history suggests that it is only when the *market* incentives were sufficient that widespread innovation and growth took hold.[11]

4.4 DATA ON IDEAS

What data do we have on ideas? At some fundamental level it is difficult to measure both the inputs to the production function for ideas and the output of that production function, the ideas themselves. At

---

[9]Sobel (1995) discusses the history of longitude in much more detail.

[10]See North and Thomas (1973).

[11]The confluence of events in the late eighteenth century is remarkable and suggestive. In addition to the beginning of the Industrial Revolution, we have the drafting of the Declaration of Independence, the U.S. Constitution and the Bill of Rights, the French Declaration of the Rights of Man and of the Citizen, and the publication of Adam Smith's *An Inquiry into the Nature and Causes of the Wealth of Nations.*

the same time, data that correspond roughly to both the inputs and the output do exist. For example, R&D is presumably a very important input into the production function for ideas. To the extent that the most important or valuable ideas are patented, patent counts may provide a simple measure of the number of ideas produced. Of course, both of these measures have their problems. Many ideas are neither patented nor produced using resources that are officially labelled as R&D. The Wal-Mart operation manual and multiplex movie theaters are good examples. In addition, a simple count of the number of patents granted in any particular year does not convey the economic value of the patents. Among the thousands of patents awarded every year, only one may be for the transistor or the laser.

Nevertheless, let us examine the patent and R&D data, keeping these caveats in mind. A patent is a legal document that describes an invention and entitles the patent owner to a monopoly over the invention for some period of time, typically 17 to 20 years. Figure 4.5 plots the number of patents awarded in every year from 1900 until 1991. The first feature apparent from the graph is the rise in the number of patents

FIGURE 4.5   **PATENTS ISSUED IN THE UNITED STATES, 1900–91**

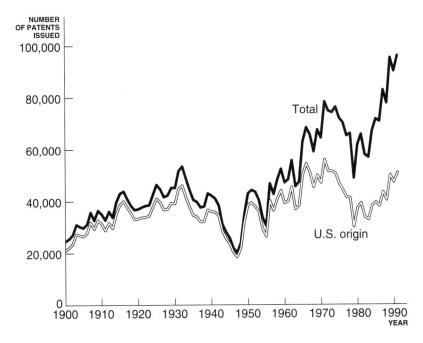

awarded. In 1900, approximately 25,000 patents were issued; in 1991, more than 96,000 patents were issued. Presumably, the number of ideas used in the U.S. economy increased substantially over the century.

This large increase masks several important features of the data, however. First, nearly half of all patents granted in 1991 were of foreign origin. Second, nearly all of the increase in patents over the last century reflects an increase in foreign patents; the number of patents awarded in the United States to U.S. residents was around 40,000 in 1915, 1950, and 1988. Does this mean that the number of new ideas generated within the United States has been relatively constant from 1915 to the present? Probably not. It is possible that the value of patents has increased or that fewer new ideas are patented. The formula for Coca-Cola, for example, is a quietly kept trade secret that has never been patented.

What about the inputs into the production of ideas? Figure 4.6 plots the number of scientists and engineers engaged in R&D from 1950 to

FIGURE 4.6   SCIENTISTS AND ENGINEERS ENGAGED IN R&D, 1950–88

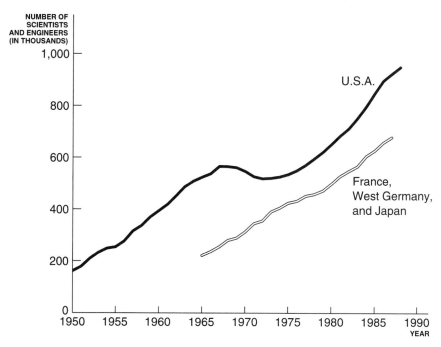

SOURCE: Jones (1995a).

1990. During this forty-year period, resources devoted to R&D increased dramatically in the United States, from less than 200,000 scientists and engineers in 1950 to nearly 1 million in 1990. A similar rise can be seen for France, West Germany, and Japan.

Not only has the *level* of resources devoted to R&D increased, but the *share* of resources devoted to R&D has also increased. The number of U.S. scientists and engineers engaged in R&D increased from about 0.25 percent of the labor force in 1950 to nearly 0.75 percent in 1990. The numbers are similarly striking for Japan, France, West Germany, and the United Kingdom. For example, the share in Japan rose from 0.2 percent in 1965 to nearly 0.8 percent in 1990.

4.5 SUMMARY

One of the main contributions of new growth theory has been to emphasize that ideas are very different from other economic goods. Ideas are nonrivalrous: once an idea is invented, it can be used by one person or by one thousand people, at no additional cost. This distinguishing feature of ideas implies that the size of the economy — its scale — plays an important role in the economics of ideas. In particular, the nonrivalry of ideas implies that production will be characterized by increasing returns to scale. In turn, the presence of increasing returns suggests that we must move away from models of perfect competition. The only reason an inventor is willing to undertake the large one-time costs of creating a new idea is because the inventor expects to be able to charge a price greater than marginal cost and earn profits.

New ideas often create benefits that the inventor is unable to capture. This is what is meant when we say that ideas are only partially excludable. The incentive to create new ideas depends on the profits that an inventor can expect to earn (the private benefit), not on the entire social benefit generated by the idea. Whether or not an idea gets created depends on the magnitude of the private benefit relative to the one-time invention costs. It is easy to see, then, how ideas that are socially very valuable may fail to be invented if private benefits and social benefits are too far apart. Patents and copyrights are legal mechanisms that attempt to bring the private benefits of invention closer in line with the social benefits. The development of such institutions — and of property rights more generally — may have played a critical role in sparking the Industrial Revolution and the sustained economic growth that has followed.

EXERCISES

1. Place the following goods on a chart like that in Figure 4.1 — i.e., classify them as rivalrous or nonrivalrous and by the extent to which they are excludable: a chicken, the trade secret for Coca-Cola, music from a compact disc, tropical rainforests, clean air, and a lighthouse that guides ships around a rocky coast.

2. Explain the role of the market and the government in providing each of the goods in the previous question.

3. Consider the following production function (similar to that used earlier for WordTalk):

$$Y = 100 * (L - F)$$

where Y is output, L is labor input, and F is a fixed amount of labor that is required before the first unit of output can be produced (like a research cost). We assume that $Y = 0$ if $L < F$. Each unit of labor L costs the wage w to hire.

(a) How much does it cost (in terms of wages) to produce 5 units of output?

(b) More generally, how much does it cost to produce *any* arbitrary amount of output, Y? That is, find the cost function $C(Y)$ that tells the minimum cost required to produce Y units of output.

(c) Show that the marginal cost dC/dY is constant (after the first unit is produced).

(d) Show that the average cost C/Y is declining.

(e) Show that if the firm charges a price P equal to marginal cost, its profits, defined as $\pi = PY - C(Y)$, will be negative regardless of the level of Y.

5 THE ENGINE OF GROWTH

> As for the Arts of Delight and Ornament, they are best promoted by the greatest number of emulators. And it is more likely that one ingenious curious man may rather be found among 4 million than among 400 persons. . . .
>
> — William Petty, *Another Essay in Political Arithmetic*, 1682 (cited in Simon 1981, p. 158)

The neoclassical growth model highlights technological progress as the engine of economic growth, and the previous chapter discussed in broad terms the economics of ideas and technology. In this chapter, we incorporate the insights from the previous chapters to develop an explicit theory of technological progress. The model we develop allows us to explore the engine of economic growth, thus addressing the second main question posed at the beginning of this book. We seek an understanding of why the advanced economies of the world, such as the United States, have grown at something like 2 percent per year for the last century. Where does the technological progress that underlies this growth come from? Why is the growth rate 2 percent per year instead of 1 percent or 10 percent? Can we expect this growth to continue, or is there some limit to economic growth?

Much of the work by economists to address these questions has been labeled *endogenous growth theory* or *new growth theory*. Instead of assuming that growth occurs because of automatic and unmodeled (exogenous) improvements in technology, the theory focuses on understanding the economic forces underlying technological progress. An important contribution of this work is the recognition that technological progress occurs as profit-maximizing firms or inventors seek out newer and better mousetraps. Adam Smith wrote that "it is not from the benevolence of the butcher, the brewer, or the baker, that we expect our dinner, but from their regard to their own interest" (Smith, 1776 [1981], pp. 26–7). Similarly, it is the possibility of earning a profit that drives firms to develop a computer that can fit in your hand, a soft drink with only a single calorie, or a way to record TV programs and movies to be replayed at your convenience. In this way, improvements in technology, and the process of economic growth itself, are understood as an endogenous outcome of the economy.

The specific theory we will develop in this chapter was constructed by Paul Romer in a series of papers, including a 1990 paper entitled "Endogeneous Technological Change."[1]

5.1 THE BASIC ELEMENTS OF THE MODEL

The Romer model endogenizes technological progress by introducing the search for new ideas by researchers interested in profiting from their inventions. The market structure and economic incentives that are at the heart of this process will be examined in detail in Section 5.2. First, though, we will outline the basic elements of the model and their implications for economic growth.

The model is designed to explain why and how the advanced countries of the world exhibit sustained growth. In contrast to the neoclassical models in earlier chapters, which could be applied to different countries, the model in this chapter describes the advanced countries of the world as a whole. Technological progress is driven by research

---

[1]The version of the Romer model that we will present in this chapter is based on Jones (1995a). There is one key difference between the two models, which will be discussed at the appropriate time. Other notable contributions to the literature on R&D-based growth models include Grossman and Helpman (1991) and Aghion and Howitt (1992). These models are sometimes called Schumpeterian growth models, because they were anticipated by the work of Joseph Schumpeter in the late 1930s and early 1940s.

and development (R&D) in the advanced world. In the next chapter we will explore the important process of technology transfer and why different economies have different levels of technology. For the moment, we will concern ourselves with how the world technological frontier is continually pushed outward.

As was the case with the Solow model, there are two main elements in the Romer model of endogenous technological change: an equation describing the production function and a set of equations describing how the inputs for the production function evolve over time. The main equations will be similar to the equations for the Solow model, with one important difference.

The aggregate production function in the Romer model describes how the capital stock, K, and labor, L_Y, combine to produce output, Y, using the stock of ideas, A:

$$Y = K^\alpha (AL_Y)^{1-\alpha}, \tag{5.1}$$

where α is a parameter between 0 and 1. For the moment, we take this production function as given; in Section 5.2, we will discuss in detail the market structure and the microfoundations of the economy that underlie this aggregate production function.

For a given level of technology, A, the production function in equation (5.1) exhibits constant returns to scale in K and L_Y. However, when we recognize that ideas (A) are also an input into production, then there are increasing returns. For example, once Steve Jobs and Steve Wozniak invented the plans for assembling personal computers, those plans (the "idea") did not need to be invented again. To double the production of personal computers, Jobs and Wozniak needed only to double the number of integrated circuits, semiconductors, etc., and find a larger garage. That is, the production function exhibits constant returns to scale with respect to the capital and labor inputs, and therefore must exhibit increasing returns with respect to all three inputs: if you double capital, labor, *and* the stock of ideas, then you will more than double output. As discussed in Chapter 4, the presence of increasing returns to scale results fundamentally from the nonrivalrous nature of ideas.

The accumulation equations for capital and labor are identical to those for the Solow model. Capital accumulates as people in the economy forego consumption at some given rate, s_K, and depreciates at the exogenous rate d:

$$\dot{K} = s_K Y - dK.$$

Labor, which is equivalent to the population, grows exponentially at some constant and exogenous rate n:

$$\frac{\dot{L}}{L} = n.$$

The key equation that is new relative to the neoclassical model is the equation describing technological progress. In the neoclassical model, the productivity term A grows exogenously at a constant rate. In the Romer model, growth in A is endogenized. How is this accomplished? According to the Romer model, $A(t)$ is the stock of knowledge or the number of ideas that have been invented over the course of history up until time t. Then, $\dot{A}$ is the number of new ideas produced at any given point in time. In the simplest version of the model, $\dot{A}$ is equal to the number of people attempting to discover new ideas, L_A, multiplied by the rate at which they discover new ideas, $\bar{\delta}$:

$$\dot{A} = \bar{\delta} L_A. \tag{5.2}$$

Labor is used either to produce new ideas or to produce output, so the economy faces the following resource constraint:

$$L_A + L_Y = L.$$

The rate at which researchers discover new ideas might simply be a constant. On the other hand, one could imagine that it depends on the stock of ideas that have already been invented. For example, perhaps the invention of ideas in the past raises the productivity of researchers in the present. In this case, $\bar{\delta}$ would be an increasing function of A. The discovery of calculus, the invention of the laser, and the development of integrated circuits are examples of ideas that have increased the productivity of later research. On the other hand, perhaps the most obvious ideas are discovered first and subsequent ideas are increasingly difficult to discover. In this case, $\bar{\delta}$ would be a decreasing function of A.

This reasoning suggests modeling the rate at which new ideas are produced as

$$\bar{\delta} = \delta A^\phi, \tag{5.3}$$

where δ and ϕ are constants. In this equation, $\phi > 0$ indicates that the productivity of research increases with the stock of ideas that have already been discovered; $\phi < 0$ corresponds to the "fishing out" case in which the fish become harder to catch over time. Finally, $\phi = 0$ indicates that the tendency for the most obvious ideas to be discovered first exactly offsets the fact that old ideas may facilitate the discovery of new ideas — i.e., the productivity of research is independent of the stock of knowledge.

It is also possible that the average productivity of research depends on the number of people searching for new ideas at any point in time. For example, perhaps duplication of effort is more likely when there are more persons engaged in research. One way of modeling this possibility is to suppose that it is really $L_A{}^\lambda$, where λ is some parameter between 0 and 1, rather than L_A that enters the production function for new ideas. This, together with equations (5.3) and (5.2), suggests focusing on the following general production function for ideas:

$$\dot{A} = \delta L_A{}^\lambda A^\phi. \tag{5.4}$$

For reasons that will become clear, we will assume that $\phi < 1$.

Equations (5.2) and (5.4) illustrate a very important aspect of modeling economic growth.[2] Individual researchers, being small relative to the economy as a whole, take $\bar{\delta}$ as given and see constant returns to research. As in equation (5.2), an individual engaged in research creates $\bar{\delta}$ new ideas. In the economy as a whole, however, the production function for ideas may not be characterized by constant returns to scale. While $\bar{\delta}$ will change by only a minuscule amount in response to the actions of a single researcher, it clearly varies with aggregate research effort.[3] For example, $\lambda < 1$ may reflect an externality associated with duplication: some of the ideas created by an individual researcher may not be new to the economy as a whole. This is analogous to congestion on a highway. Each driver ignores the fact that his or her presence makes it slightly harder for other drivers to get where they are going. The effect of any

---

[2]This modeling technique will be explored again in Chapter 8 in the context of "AK" models of growth.

[3]Notice that the exact expression for $\bar{\delta}$, incorporating both duplication and knowledge spillovers, is $\bar{\delta} = \delta L_A{}^{\lambda-1} A^\phi$.

single driver is negligible, but summed across all drivers, the effects can be important.

Similarly, the presence of A^ϕ is treated as external to the individual agent. Consider the case of $\phi > 0$, reflecting a positive knowledge spillover in research. The gains to society from the theory of gravitation far outweighed the benefit that Isaac Newton was able to capture. Much of the knowledge he created "spilled over" to future researchers. Of course, Newton himself also benefited from the knowledge created by previous scientists such as Kepler, as he recognized in the famous statement, "If I have seen farther than others, it is because I was standing on the shoulders of giants." With this in mind, we might refer to the externality associated with $\phi > 0$ as the "standing on shoulders" effect, and by extension, the externality associated with $\lambda < 1$ as the "stepping on toes" effect.

5.1.1 GROWTH IN THE ROMER MODEL

What is the growth rate in this model along a balanced growth path? Provided a constant fraction of the population is employed producing ideas (which we will show to be the case below), the model follows the neoclassical model in predicting that all per capita growth is due to technological progress. Letting lower-case letters denote per capita variables, and letting g_x denote the growth rate of some variable x along the balanced growth path, it is easy to show that

$$g_y = g_k = g_A.$$

That is, per capita output, the capital-labor ratio, and the stock of ideas must all grow at the same rate along a balanced growth path.[4] If there is no technological progress in the model, then there is no growth.

Therefore, the important question is "What is the rate of technological progress along a balanced growth path?" The answer to this question is found by rewriting the production function for ideas, equation (5.4).

---

[4]To see this, follow the arguments we made in deriving equation (2.10) in Chapter 2. Intuitively, the capital-output ratio must be constant along a balanced growth path. Recognizing this fact, the production function implies that y and k must grow at the same rate as A.

Dividing both sides of this equation by A yields

$$\frac{\dot{A}}{A} = \delta \frac{L_A{}^\lambda}{A^{1-\phi}}. \tag{5.5}$$

Along a balanced growth path, $\frac{\dot{A}}{A} \equiv g_A$ is constant. But this growth rate will be constant if and only if the numerator and the denominator of the right-hand side of equation (5.5) grow at the same rate. Taking logs and derivatives of both sides of this equation,

$$0 = \lambda \frac{\dot{L}_A}{L_A} - (1 - \phi)\frac{\dot{A}}{A}. \tag{5.6}$$

Along a balanced growth path, the growth rate of the number of researchers must be equal to the growth rate of the population — if it were higher, the number of researchers would eventually exceed the population, which is impossible. That is, $\dot{L}_A/L_A = n$. Substituting this into (5.6) yields

$$g_A = \frac{\lambda n}{1 - \phi}. \tag{5.7}$$

Thus the long-run growth rate of this economy is determined by the parameters of the production function for ideas and the rate of growth of researchers, which is ultimately given by the population growth rate.

Several features of this equation deserve comment. First, what is the intuition for the equation? The intuition is most easily seen by considering the special case in which $\lambda = 1$ and $\phi = 0$ so that the productivity of researchers is the constant δ. In this case, there is no duplication problem in research and the productivity of a researcher today is independent of the stock of ideas that have been discovered in the past. The production function for ideas looks like

$$\dot{A} = \delta L_A.$$

Now suppose that the number of people engaged in the search for ideas is constant. Because δ is also constant, this economy generates a constant number of new ideas, δL_A, each period. To be more concrete, let's suppose $\delta L_A = 100$. The economy begins with some stock of ideas, A_0, generated by previous discoveries. Initially, the 100 new ideas per period may be a large fraction of the existing stock, A_0. Over time, though, the stock grows, and the 100 new ideas becomes a smaller and smaller fraction of the existing stock. Therefore, the *growth rate* of the stock of ideas falls over time, eventually approaching zero. Notice, however, that technological progress never ceases. The economy is always creating 100 new ideas. It is simply that these 100 new ideas shrink in comparison with the accumulated stock of ideas.

In order to generate growth, the number of new ideas must be expanding over time. This occurs if the number of researchers is increasing — for example, because of world population growth. More researchers mean more ideas, sustaining growth in the model. In this case, the growth in ideas is clearly related to the growth in population, which explains the presence of population growth in equation (5.7).

It is interesting to compare this result to the effect of population growth in the neoclassical growth model. There, for example, a higher population growth rate reduces the level of income along a balanced growth path. More people means that more capital is needed to keep K/L constant, but capital runs into diminishing returns. Here, an important additional effect exists. People are the key input to the creative process. A larger population generates more ideas, and because ideas are nonrivalrous, everyone in the economy benefits.

What evidence can be presented to support the contention that the per capita growth rate of the world economy depends on population growth? First, notice that this particular implication of the model is very difficult to test. We have already indicated that this model of the engine of growth is meant to describe the advanced countries of the world taken as a whole. Thus, we cannot use evidence on population growth *across* countries to test the model. In fact, we have already presented one of the most compelling pieces of evidence in Chapter 4. Recall the plot in Figure 4.4 of world population growth rates over the last 2,000 years. Sustained and rapid population growth is a rather recent phenomenon, just as is sustained and rapid growth in per capita output. Increases in the rate of population growth from the very low rate observed over most of history occurred at roughly the same time as the Industrial Revolution.

The result that the growth rate of the economy is tied to the growth rate of the population implies another seemingly strong result: if the population (or at least the number of researchers) stops growing, long-run growth ceases. What do we make of this prediction? Rephrasing the question slightly, if research effort in the world were constant over time, would economic growth eventually grind to a halt? This model suggests that it would. A constant research effort cannot continue the proportional increases in the stock of ideas needed to generate long-run growth.

Actually, there is one special case in which a constant research effort can sustain long-run growth, and this brings us to our second main comment about the model. The production function for ideas considered in the original Romer (1990) paper assumes that $\lambda = 1$ and $\phi = 1$. That is,

$$\dot{A} = \delta L_A A.$$

Rewriting the equation slightly, we can see that this version of the Romer model *will* generate sustained growth in the presence of a constant research effort:

$$\frac{\dot{A}}{A} = \delta L_A. \tag{5.8}$$

In this case, Romer assumes that the productivity of research is proportional to the existing stock of ideas: $\bar{\delta} = \delta A$. With this assumption, the productivity of researchers grows over time, even if the number of researchers is constant.

The advantage of this specification, however, is also its drawback. World research effort has increased enormously over the last forty years and even over the last century (see Figure 4.6 in Chapter 4 for a reminder of this fact). Since L_A is growing rapidly over time, the original Romer formulation in equation (5.8) predicts that the growth rate of the advanced economies should also have risen rapidly over the last forty years or the last century. We know this is far from the truth. The average growth rate of the U.S. economy, for example, has been very close to 1.8 percent per year for the last hundred years. This easily rejected prediction of the original Romer formulation is avoided by requiring that ϕ is less than one, which returns us to the results associated with equation (5.7).[5]

Notice that nothing in this reasoning rules out increasing returns in research or positive knowledge spillovers. The knowledge spillover parameter, ϕ, may be positive and quite large. What the reasoning points

---

[5] This point is made in Jones (1995a).

out is that the somewhat arbitrary case of $\phi = 1$ is strongly rejected by empirical observation.[6]

Our last comment about the growth implications of this model of technology is that the results are similar to the neoclassical model in one very important way. In the neoclassical model, changes in government policy and changes in the investment rate have no long-run effect on economic growth. This result was not surprising once we recognized that all growth in the neoclassical model was due to exogenous technological progress. In this model with endogenous technological progress, however, we have the same result. The long-run growth rate is invariant to changes in the investment rate, and even to changes in the share of the population that is employed in research. This is seen by noting that none of the parameters in equation (5.7) is affected when, say, the investment rate or the R&D share of labor is changed. Instead, these policies affect the growth rate along a transition path to the new steady state altering the *level* of income. That is, even after we endogenize technology in this model, the long-run growth rate cannot be manipulated by policy makers using conventional policies such as subsidies to R&D.

5.1.2 GROWTH EFFECTS VERSUS LEVEL EFFECTS

The fact that standard policies cannot affect long-run growth is *not* a feature of the original Romer model, nor of many other idea-based growth models that followed, including Grossman and Helpman (1991) and Aghion and Howitt (1992). Much of the theoretical work in new growth theory has sought to develop models in which policy changes *can* have effects on long-run growth.

The idea-based models in which changes in policy can permanently increase the growth rate of the economy all rely on the assumption that $\phi = 1$, or its equivalent. As shown above, this assumption generates the counterfactual prediction that growth rates should accelerate over time with a growing population. Jones (1995a) generalized these models to the case of $\phi < 1$ to eliminate this defect, and showed the somewhat

---

[6]The same evidence also rules out values of $\phi > 1$. Such values would generate accelerating growth rates even with a constant population!

surprising implication that this eliminates the long-run growth effects of policy as well. We will discuss these issues in more detail in Chapter 8.

5.1.3 COMPARATIVE STATICS: A PERMANENT INCREASE IN THE R&D SHARE

What happens to the advanced economies of the world if the share of the population searching for new ideas increases permanently? For example, suppose there is a government subsidy for R&D that increases the fraction of the labor force doing research.

An important feature of the model we have just developed is that many policy changes (or comparative statics) can be analyzed with techniques we have already developed. Why? Notice that technological progress in the model can be analyzed by itself — it doesn't depend on capital or output, but only on the labor force and the share of the population devoted to research. Once the growth rate of A is constant, the model behaves just like the Solow model with exogenous technological progress. Therefore, our analysis proceeds in two steps. First, we consider what happens to technological progress and to the stock of ideas after the increase in R&D intensity occurs. Second, we analyze the model as we did the Solow model, in steps familiar from Chapter 2. Before we proceed, it is worth noting that the analysis of changes that do not affect technology, such as an increase in the investment rate, is exactly like the analysis of the Solow model.

Now consider what happens if the share of the population engaged in research increases permanently. To simplify things slightly, let's assume that $\lambda = 1$ and $\phi = 0$ again; none of the results are qualitatively affected by this assumption. It is helpful to rewrite equation (5.5) as

$$\frac{\dot{A}}{A} = \delta \frac{s_R L}{A},$$

(5.9)

where s_R is defined as the share of the population engaged in R&D — i.e., $L_A = s_R L$.

Figure 5.1 shows what happens to technological progress when s_R increases permanently to s_R', assuming the economy begins in steady state. In steady state, the economy grows along a balanced growth path at the rate of technological progress, g_A, which happens to equal the rate of population growth under our simplifying assumptions. The ratio L_A/A is therefore equal to g_A/δ. Suppose the increase in s_R occurs at

FIGURE 5.1   TECHNOLOGICAL PROGRESS: AN INCREASE IN THE R&D SHARE

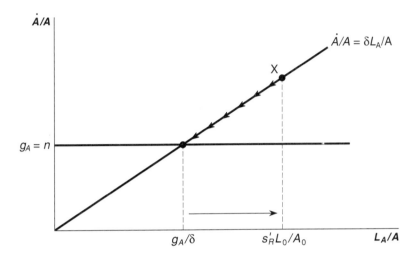

time $t = 0$. With a population of L_0, the number of researchers increases as s_R increases so that the ratio L_A/A jumps to a higher level. The additional researchers produce an increased number of new ideas, so the growth rate of technology is also higher at this point. This situation corresponds to the point labelled "X" in the figure. At X, technological progress $\dot{A}/A$ exceeds population growth n, so the ratio L_A/A declines over time, as indicated by the arrows. As this ratio declines, the rate of technological change gradually falls also, until the economy returns to the balanced growth path where $g_A = n$. Therefore, a permanent increase in the share of the population devoted to research raises the rate of technological progress temporarily, but not in the long run. This behavior is depicted in Figure 5.2.

What happens to the level of technology in this economy? Figure 5.3 answers this question. The level of technology is growing along a balanced growth path at rate g_A until time $t = 0$. At this time, the growth rate increases and the level of technology rises faster than before. Over time, however, the growth rate falls until it returns to g_A. The *level* of technology is permanently higher as a result of the permanent increase in R&D. Notice that a permanent increase in s_R in the Romer model generates transition dynamics that are qualitatively similar to the dynamics generated by an increase in the investment rate in the Solow model.

FIGURE 5.2 $\dot{A}/A$ OVER TIME

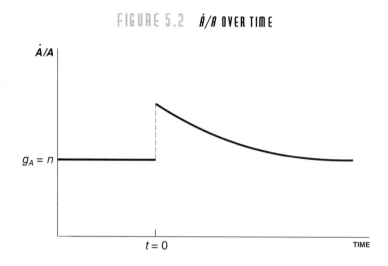

Now that we know what happens to technology over time, we can analyze the remainder of the model in a Solow framework. The long-run growth rate of the model is constant, so much of the algebra that we used in analyzing the Solow model applies. For example, the ratio y/A is constant along a balanced growth path and is given by an equation similar to equation (2.13):

$$\left(\frac{y}{A}\right)^* = \left(\frac{s_K}{n + g_A + d}\right)^{\alpha/(1-\alpha)} (1 - s_R). \qquad (5.10)$$

FIGURE 5.3   THE LEVEL OF TECHNOLOGY OVER TIME

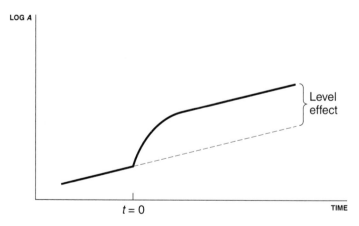

The only difference is the presence of the term $1 - s_R$, which adjusts for the difference between output per worker, L_Y, and output per capita, L.

Notice that along a balanced growth path, equation (5.9) can be solved for the level of A in terms of the labor force:

$$A = \frac{\delta s_R L}{g_A}.$$

Combining this equation with (5.10), we get

$$y^*(t) = \left(\frac{s_K}{n + g_A + d} \right)^{\alpha/(1-\alpha)} (1 - s_R) \frac{\delta s_R}{g_A} L(t). \qquad (5.11)$$

In this simple version of the model, per capita output is proportional to the population of the (world) economy along a balanced growth path. In other words, the model exhibits a *scale effect* in levels: a larger world economy will be a richer world economy. This scale effect arises fundamentally from the nonrivalrous nature of ideas: a larger economy provides a larger market for an idea, raising the return to research (a demand effect). In addition, a more populous world economy simply has more potential creators of ideas in the first place (a supply effect).

The other terms in equation (5.11) are readily interpreted. The first term is familiar from the original Solow model. Economies that invest more in capital will be richer, for example. Two terms involve the share of labor devoted to research, s_R. The first time s_R appears, it enters negatively to reflect the fact that more researchers mean fewer workers producing output. The second time, it enters positively to reflect the fact that more researchers mean more ideas, which increases the productivity of the economy.

5.2 THE ECONOMICS OF THE MODEL

The first half of this chapter has analyzed the Romer model without discussing the economics underlying the model. A number of economists in the 1960s developed models with similar macroeconomic features.[7] However, the development of the microfoundations of such models had to wait until the 1980s when economists better understood how to

---

[7] For example, Uzawa (1965), Phelps (1966), Shell (1967), and Nordhaus (1969).

model imperfect competition in a general equilibrium setting.[8] In fact, one of the important contributions of Romer (1990) was to explain exactly how to construct a mini-economy of profit-maximizing agents that endogenizes technological progress. The intuition behind this insight was developed in Chapter 4. Developing the mathematics is the subject of the remainder of this section. Because this section is somewhat difficult, some readers may wish to skip to Section 5.3.

The Romer economy consists of three sectors: a final-goods sector, an intermediate-goods sector, and a research sector. The reason for two of the sectors should be clear: some firms must produce output and some firms must produce ideas. The reason for the intermediate-goods sector is related to the presence of increasing returns discussed in Chapter 4. Each of these sectors will be discussed in turn. Briefly, the research sector creates new ideas, which take the form of new varieties of capital goods — new computer chips, fax machines, or printing presses. The research sector sells the exclusive right to produce a specific capital good to an intermediate-goods firm. The intermediate-goods firm, as a monopolist, manufactures the capital good and sells it to the final-goods sector, which produces output.

5.2.1 THE FINAL-GOODS SECTOR

The final-goods sector of the Romer economy is very much like the final-goods sector of the Solow model. It consists of a large number of perfectly competitive firms that combine labor and capital to produce a homogeneous output good, Y. The production function is specified in a slightly different way, though, to reflect the fact that there is more than one capital good in the model:

$$Y = L_Y^{1-\alpha} \sum_{j=1}^{A} x_j^{\alpha}.$$

Output, Y, is produced using labor, L_Y, and a number of different capital goods, x_j, which we will also call "intermediate goods." At any point in time, A measures the number of capital goods that are available to be

---

[8]Key steps in this understanding were accomplished by Spence (1976), Dixit and Stiglitz (1977), and Ethier (1982).

used in the final-goods sector, and firms in the final-goods sector take this number as given. Inventions or ideas in the model correspond to the creation of new capital goods that can be used by the final-goods sector to produce output.

Notice that this production function can be rewritten as

$$Y = L_Y^{1-\alpha} x_1^{\alpha} + L_Y^{1-\alpha} x_2^{\alpha} + \cdots + L_Y^{1-\alpha} x_A^{\alpha},$$

and it is easy to see that, for a given A, the production function exhibits constant returns to scale; doubling the amount of labor and the amount of each capital good will exactly double output.

It turns out for technical reasons to be easier to analyze the model if we replace the summation in the production function with an integral:

$$Y = L_Y^{1-\alpha} \int_0^A x_j^{\alpha} \, dj.$$

Then, A measures the range of capital goods that are available to the final-goods sector, and this range is the interval on the real line $[0, A]$. The basic interpretation of this equation, though, is unaffected by this technicality.

With constant returns to scale, the number of firms cannot be pinned down, so we will assume there are a large number of identical firms producing final output and that perfect competition prevails in this sector. We will also normalize the price of the final output, Y, to unity.

Firms in the final-goods sector have to decide how much labor and how much of each capital good to utilize in producing output. They do this by solving the profit-maximization problem:

$$\max_{L_Y, x_j} L_Y^{1-\alpha} \int_0^A x_j^{\alpha} \, dj - wL_Y - \int_0^A p_j x_j \, dj,$$

where p_j is the rental price for capital good j and w is the wage paid for labor. The first-order conditions characterizing the solution to this problem are

$$w = (1 - \alpha) \frac{Y}{L_Y} \tag{5.12}$$

and

$$p_j = \alpha L_Y^{1-\alpha} x_j^{\alpha-1}, \tag{5.13}$$

where this second condition applies to each capital good j. The first condition says that firms hire labor until the marginal product of labor equals the wage. The second condition says the same thing, but for capital goods: firms rent capital goods until the marginal product of each kind of capital equals the rental price, p_j. To see the intuition for these equations, suppose the marginal product of a capital good were higher than its rental price. Then the firm should rent another unit — the output produced will more than pay for the rental price. If the marginal product is below the rental price, then the firm can increase profits by reducing the amount of capital used.

5.2.2 THE INTERMEDIATE-GOODS SECTOR

The intermediate-goods sector consists of monopolists who produce the capital goods that are sold to the final-goods sector. These firms gain their monopoly power by purchasing the design for a specific capital good from the research sector. Because of patent protection, only one firm manufactures each capital good.

Once the design for a particular capital good has been purchased (a fixed cost), the intermediate-goods firm produces the capital good with a very simple production function: one unit of raw capital can be automatically translated into one unit of the capital good. The profit maximization problem for an intermediate goods firm is then

$$\max_{x_j} \pi_j = p_j(x_j)x_j - rx_j,$$

where $p_j(x)$ is the demand function for the capital good given in equation (5.13). The first-order condition for this problem, dropping the j subscripts, is

$$p'(x)x + p(x) - r = 0.$$

Rewriting this equation we get

$$p'(x)\frac{x}{p} + 1 = \frac{r}{p},$$

which implies that

$$p = \frac{1}{1 + \frac{p'(x)x}{p}} r.$$

Finally, the elasticity, $p'(x)x/p$, can be calculated from the demand curve in equation (5.13). It is equal to $\alpha - 1$, so the intermediate-goods firm charges a price that is simply a markup over marginal cost, r:

$$p = \frac{1}{\alpha}r.$$

This is the solution for each monopolist, so that all capital goods sell for the same price. Because the demand functions in equation (5.13) are also the same, each capital good is employed by the final-goods firms in the same amount: $x_j = x$. Therefore, each capital-goods firm earns the same profit. With some algebra, one can show that this profit is given by

$$\pi = \alpha(1 - \alpha)\frac{Y}{A}. \tag{5.14}$$

Finally, the total demand for capital from the intermediate-goods firms must equal the total capital stock in the economy:

$$\int_0^A x_j dj = K.$$

Since the capital goods are each used in the same amount, x, this equation can be used to determine x:

$$x = \frac{K}{A}. \tag{5.15}$$

The final-goods production function can be rewritten, using the fact that $x_j = x$, as

$$Y = AL_Y^{1-\alpha}x^\alpha,$$

and substituting from equation (5.15) reveals that

$$Y = AL_Y^{1-\alpha}A^{-\alpha}K^\alpha$$
$$= K^\alpha(AL_Y)^{1-\alpha}. \tag{5.16}$$

That is, we see that the production technology for the final-goods sector generates the same aggregate production function used throughout this book. In particular, this is the aggregate production function used in equation (5.1).

5.2.3 THE RESEARCH SECTOR

Much of the analysis of the research sector has already been provided. The research sector is essentially like gold mining in the wild West in the mid-nineteenth century. Anyone is free to "prospect" for ideas, and the reward for prospecting is the discovery of a "nugget" that can be sold. Ideas in this model are designs for new capital goods: a faster computer chip, a method for genetically altering corn to make it more resistant to pests, or a new way to organize movie theaters. These designs can be thought of as instructions that explain how to transform a unit of raw capital into a unit of a new capital good. New designs are discovered according to equation (5.4).

When a new design is discovered, the inventor receives a patent from the government for the exclusive right to produce the new capital good. (To simplify the analysis, we assume that the patent lasts forever.) The inventor sells the patent to an intermediate-goods firm and uses the proceeds to consume and save, just like any other agent in the model. But what is the price of a patent for a new design?

We assume that anyone can bid for the patent. How much will a potential bidder be willing to pay? The answer is the present discounted value of the profits to be earned by an intermediate-goods firm. Any less, and someone would be willing to bid higher; any more, and no one would be willing to bid. Let P_A be the price of a new design, this present discounted value. How does P_A change over time? The answer lies in an extremely useful line of reasoning in economics and finance called the method of *arbitrage*.

The arbitrage argument goes as follows. Suppose I have some money to invest for one period. I have two options. First, I can put the money in the "bank" (in this model, this is equivalent to purchasing a unit of capital) and earn the interest rate r. Alternatively, I can purchase a patent for one period, earn the profits that period, and then sell the patent. In equilibrium, it must be the case that the rate of return from both of these investments is the same. If not, everyone would jump at the more profitable investment, driving its return down. Mathematically, the *arbitrage equation* states that the returns are the same:

$$rP_A = \pi + \dot{P}_A. \tag{5.17}$$

The left-hand side of this equation is the interest earned from investing P_A in the bank; the right-hand side is the profits plus the capital gain or loss that results from the change in the price of the patent. These two must be equal in equilibrium.

Rewriting equation (5.17) slightly,

$$r = \frac{\pi}{P_A} + \frac{\dot{P_A}}{P_A}.$$

Along a balanced growth path, r is constant.[9] Therefore, π/P_A must be constant also, which means that π and P_A have to grow at the same rate; this rate turns out to be the population growth rate, n.[10] Therefore, the arbitrage equation implies that

$$P_A = \frac{\pi}{r - n}. \qquad (5.18)$$

This equation gives the price of a patent along a balanced growth path.

5.2.4 SOLVING THE MODEL

We have now described the market structure and the microeconomics underlying the basic equations given in Section 5.1. The model is some-what complicated, but several features that were discussed in Chapter 4 are worth noting. First, the aggregate production function exhibits in-creasing returns. There are constant returns to K and L, but increasing returns once we note that ideas, A, are also an input to production. Second, the increasing returns require imperfect competition. This ap-pears in the model in the intermediate-goods sector. Firms in this sector are monopolists, and capital goods sell at a price that is greater than marginal cost. However, the profits earned by these firms are extracted by the inventors, and these profits simply compensate the inventors for the time they spend "prospecting" for new designs. This framework is called *monopolistic competition*. There are no economic profits in the model; all rents compensate some factor input. Finally, once we depart from the world of perfect competition there is no reason to think that

---

[9]The interest rate r is constant for the usual reasons. It will be the price at which the supply of capital is equal to the demand for capital, and will be proportional to Y/K.
[10]To see this, recall from equation (5.14) that π is proportional to Y/A. Per capita output, y, and A grow at the same rate, so that Y/A will grow at the rate of population growth.

markets yield the "best of all possible worlds." This last point is one
that we develop more carefully in the next section.

We have already solved for the growth rate of the economy in steady
state. The part of the model that remains to be solved is the allocation
of labor between research and the final-goods sector. What fraction of
the population works where?

Once again, the concept of arbitrage enters. It must be the case that at
the margin, individuals in this simplified model are indifferent between
working in the final-goods sector and working in the research sector.
Labor working in the final-goods sector earns a wage that is equal to its
marginal product in that sector, as given in equation (5.12):

$$w_Y = (1 - \alpha)\frac{Y}{L_Y}.$$

Researchers earn a wage based on the value of the designs they discover. We will assume that researchers take their productivity in the
research sector, $\bar{\delta}$, as given. They do not recognize that productivity
falls as more labor enters because of duplication, and they do not inter-
nalize the knowledge spillover associated with ϕ. Therefore, the wage
earned by labor in the research sector is equal to its marginal product,
$\bar{\delta}$, multiplied by the value of the new ideas created, P_A:

$$w_R = \bar{\delta}P_A.$$

Because there is free entry into both the research sector and the final
goods sector, these wages must be the same: $w_Y = w_R$. This condition,
with some algebra shown in the appendix to this chapter, reveals that
the share of the population that works in the research sector, s_R, is given
by

$$s_R = \frac{1}{1 + \frac{r-n}{\alpha g_A}}. \tag{5.19}$$

Notice that the faster the economy grows (the higher is g_A), the higher
the fraction of the population that works in research. The higher the
discount rate that applies to current profits to get the present discounted
value $(r - n)$, the lower the fraction working in research.[11]

---

[11]One can eliminate the interest rate from this equation by noting that $r = \alpha^2 Y/K$ and
getting the capital-output ratio from the capital accumulation equation: $Y/K = (n + g + d)/s_K$.

With some algebra, one can show that the interest rate in this economy is given by $r = \alpha^2 Y/K$. Notice that this is *less* than the marginal product of capital, which from equation (5.16) is the familiar $\alpha Y/K$. This difference reflects an important point. In the Solow model with perfect competition and constant returns to scale, all factors are paid their marginal products: $r = \alpha Y/K$, $w = (1 - \alpha)Y/L$, and therefore $rK + wL = Y$. In the Romer model, however, production in the economy is characterized by increasing returns and all factors cannot be paid their marginal products. This is clear from the Solow example just given: because $rK + wL = Y$, there is no output in the Solow economy remaining to compensate individuals for their effort in creating new A. *This* is what necessitates imperfect competition in the model. Here, capital is paid less than its marginal product, and the remainder is used to compensate researchers for the creation of new ideas.

5.3 OPTIMAL R&D

Is the share of the population that works in research optimal? In general, the answer to this question in the Romer model is no. In this case, the markets do not induce the right amount of labor to work in research. Why not? Where does Adam Smith's invisible hand go wrong?

There are three distortions to research in the model that cause s_R to differ from its optimal level. Two of the distortions are easy to see from the production function for ideas. First, the market values research according to the stream of profits that are earned from the new design. What the market misses, though, is that the new invention may affect the productivity of future research. Recall that $\phi > 0$ implies that the productivity of research increases with the stock of ideas. The problem here is one of a missing market: researchers are not compensated for their contribution toward improving the productivity of future researchers. For example, subsequent generations did not reward Isaac Newton sufficiently for inventing calculus. Therefore, with $\phi > 0$, there is a tendency, other things being equal, for the market to provide too little research. This distortion is often called a "knowledge spillover" because some of the knowledge created "spills over" to other researchers. This is the "standing on shoulders" effect referred to earlier. In this sense, it is very much like a classic positive externality: if the bees that a farmer raises for honey provide an extra benefit to the community that the farmer doesn't capture (they pollinate the apple trees in the surrounding area), the market will underprovide honey bees.[12]

The second distortion, the "stepping on toes" effect, is also a classic externality. It occurs because researchers do not take into account the fact that they lower research productivity through duplication when λ is less than 1. In this case, however, the externality is negative. Therefore, the market tends to provide too much research, other things being equal.

Finally, the third distortion can be called a "consumer-surplus effect." The intuition for this distortion is simple and can be seen by considering a standard monopoly problem, as in Figure 5.4. An inventor of a new design captures the monopoly profit shown in the figure. However, the potential gain to society from inventing the good is the entire consumer-surplus triangle above the marginal cost of production (MC). The incentive to innovate, the monopoly profit, is less than the gain to society, and this effect tends to generate too little innovation, other things being equal.

FIGURE 5.4   THE "CONSUMER-SURPLUS EFFECT"

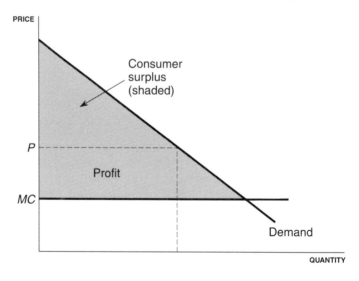

_____

[12]On the other hand, if $\phi < 0$, then the reverse could be true.

In practice, these distortions can be very large. Consider the consumer surplus associated with basic inventions such as the cure for malaria or cholera or the discovery of calculus. For these inventions, associated with "basic science," the knowledge spillovers and the consumer-surplus effects are generally felt to be so large that the government funds basic research in universities and research centers.

These distortions may also be important even for R&D undertaken by firms. Consider the consumer surplus benefits from the invention of the telephone, electric power, the laser, and the transistor. A substantial literature in economics, led by Zvi Griliches, Edwin Mansfield, and others, seeks to estimate the "social" rate of return to research performed by firms. Griliches (1991) reviews this literature and finds social rates of return on the order of 40 to 60 percent, far exceeding private rates of return. As an empirical matter, this suggests that the positive externalities of research outweigh the negative externalities so that the market, even in the presence of the modern patent system, tends to provide too little research.

A final comment on imperfect competition and monopolies is in order. Classical economic theory argues that monopolies are bad for welfare and efficiency because they create "deadweight losses" in the economy. This reasoning underlies regulations designed to prevent firms from pricing above marginal cost. In contrast, the economics of ideas suggests that it is critical that firms be allowed to price above marginal cost. It is exactly this wedge that provides the profits that are the incentive for firms to innovate. In deciding antitrust issues, modern regulation of imperfect competition has to weigh the deadweight losses against the incentive to innovate.

5.4 SUMMARY

Technological progress is the engine of economic growth. In this chapter, we have endogenized the process by which technological change occurs. Instead of "manna from heaven," technological progress arises as individuals seek out new ideas in an effort to capture some of the social gain these new ideas generate in the form of profit. Better mousetraps get invented and marketed because people will pay a premium for a better way to catch mice.

In Chapter 4, we showed that the nonrivalrous nature of ideas implies that production is characterized by increasing returns to scale. In this chapter, this implication served to illustrate the general importance of scale in the economy. Specifically, the growth rate of world technology is tied to the growth rate of the population. A larger number of researchers can create a larger number of ideas, and it is this general principle that generates per capita growth.

As in the Solow model, comparative statics in this model (such as an increase in the investment rate or an increase in the share of the labor force engaged in R&D) generate *level effects* rather than long-run growth effects. For example, a government subsidy that increases the share of labor in research will typically increase the growth rate of the economy, but only temporarily, as the economy transits to a higher level of income.

The results of this chapter match up nicely with the historical evidence documented in Chapter 4. Consider broadly the history of economic growth in reverse chronological order. The Romer model is clearly meant to describe the evolution of technology since the establishment of intellectual property rights. It is the presence of patents and copyrights that enables inventors to earn profits to cover the initial costs of developing new ideas. In the last century (or two), the world economy has witnessed sustained, rapid growth in population, technology, and per capita income never before seen in history.

Consider how the model economy would behave in the absence of property rights. In this case, innovators would be unable to earn the profits that encourage them to undertake research in the first place, so that no research would take place. With no research, no new ideas would be created, technology would be constant, and there would be no per capita growth in the economy. Broadly speaking, just such a situation prevailed in the world prior to the Industrial Revolution.[13]

Finally, a large body of research suggests that social returns to innovation remain well above private returns. Although the "prizes" that the market offers to potential innovators are substantial, these prizes

---

[13]There were, of course, very notable scientific and technological advances before 1760, but these were intermittent and there was little sustained growth. What did occur might be attributed to individual curiosity, government rewards, or public funding (such as the prize for the chronometer and the support for astronomical observatories).

still fall far short of the total gain to society from innovations. This gap between social and private returns suggests that large gains are still available from the creation of new mechanisms designed to encourage research. Mechanisms like the patent system are themselves ideas, and there is no reason to think the best ideas have already been discovered.

APPENDIX: SOLVING FOR THE R&D SHARE

The share of the population that works in research, s_R, is obtained by setting the wage in the final-goods sector equal to the wage in research:

$$\bar{\delta} P_A = (1 - \alpha) \frac{Y}{L_Y}.$$

Substituting for P_A from equation (5.18),

$$\bar{\delta} \frac{\pi}{r - n} = (1 - \alpha) \frac{Y}{L_Y}.$$

Recall that π is proportional to Y/A in equation (5.14):

$$\frac{\bar{\delta}}{r - n} \alpha (1 - \alpha) \frac{Y}{A} = (1 - \alpha) \frac{Y}{L_Y}.$$

Several terms cancel, leaving

$$\frac{\alpha}{r - n} \frac{\bar{\delta}}{A} = \frac{1}{L_Y}.$$

Finally, notice that $\dot{A}/A = \bar{\delta} L_A/A$ so that $\bar{\delta}/A = g_A/L_A$ along a balanced growth path. With this substitution,

$$\frac{\alpha g_A}{r - n} = \frac{L_A}{L_Y}.$$

Notice that L_A/L_Y is just $s_R/(1 - s_R)$. Solving the equation for s_R then reveals

$$s_R = \frac{1}{1 + \frac{r-n}{\alpha g_A}},$$

as reported in equation (5.19).

EXERCISES

1. *An increase in the productivity of research.* Suppose there is a one-time increase in the productivity of research, represented by an increase in δ in Figure 5.1. What happens to the growth rate and the level of technology over time?

2. *Too much of a good thing?* Consider the level of per capita income along a balanced growth path given by equation (5.11). Find the value for s_R that maximizes output per worker along a balanced growth path for this example. Why is it possible to do too much R&D according to this criterion?

3. *The future of economic growth* (from Jones (1997b)). Recall from Figure 4.6 and the discussion surrounding this figure in Chapter 4 that the number of scientists and engineers engaged in R&D has been growing faster than the rate of population growth in the advanced economies of the world. To take some plausible numbers, assume population growth is 1 percent and the growth rate of researchers is 3 percent per year. Assume that $\dot{A}/A$ has been constant at about 2 percent per year. (Why?)

   (a) Using equation (5.6), calculate an estimate of $\lambda/(1 - \phi)$.

   (b) Using this estimate and equation (5.7), calculate an estimate of the long-run steady-state growth rate of the world economy.

   (c) Why are these numbers different? What do they mean?

   (d) Does the fact that many developing countries are starting to engage in R&D change this calculation?

4. *The share of the surplus appropriated by inventors* (from Kremer (1996)). In Figure 5.4, find the ratio of the profit captured by the monopolist to the total potential consumer surplus available if the good were priced at marginal cost. Assume that marginal cost is constant at c and the demand curve is linear: $Q = a - bP$, where a, b, and c are positive constants with $a - bc > 0$.

6 A SIMPLE MODEL OF GROWTH AND DEVELOPMENT

The neoclassical growth model allows us to think about why some countries are rich while others are poor, taking technology and factor accumulation as exogenous. The Romer model provides the microeconomic underpinnings for a model of the technological frontier and why technology grows over time. It answers in detail our questions concerning the "engine of growth." In this chapter, we address the next logical question, which is how technologies diffuse across countries, and why the technology used in some countries is so much more advanced than the technology used in others.

6.1 THE BASIC MODEL

The framework we develop builds naturally on the Romer model of technology discussed in Chapter 5. The component that we add to the model is an avenue for technology transfer. We endogenize the mechanism by which different countries achieve the ability to use various intermediate capital goods.

As with the Romer model, countries produce a homogeneous output good, Y, using labor, L, and a range of capital goods, x_j. The "number" of capital goods that workers can use is limited by their skill level, h:[1]

$$Y = L^{1-\alpha} \int_0^h x_j{}^\alpha \, dj. \tag{6.1}$$

Once again, think of the integral as a sum. A worker with a high skill level can use more capital goods than a worker with a low skill level. For example, a highly skilled worker may be able to use computerized machine tools unavailable to workers below a certain skill level.

In Chapter 5, we focused on the invention of new capital goods as an engine of growth for the world economy. Here, we will have the opposite focus. We assume that we are examining the economic performance of a single small country, potentially far removed from the technological frontier. This country grows by learning to utilize the more advanced capital goods that are already available in the rest of the world. Whereas the model in Chapter 5 can be thought of as applying to the OECD or the world as a whole, this model is best applied to a specific economy.

One unit of any intermediate capital good can be produced with one unit of raw capital. To simplify the setup, we assume this transformation is effortless and can also be undone effortlessly. Thus,

$$\int_0^{h(t)} x_j(t) \, dj = K(t), \tag{6.2}$$

that is, the total quantity of capital goods of all types used in production is equal to the total supply of raw capital. Intermediate goods are treated symmetrically throughout the model, so that $x_j = x$ for all j. This fact, together with equation (6.2) and the production function in (6.1), implies that the aggregate production technology for this economy takes the familiar Cobb-Douglas form

$$Y = K^\alpha (hL)^{1-\alpha}. \tag{6.3}$$

Notice that an individual's skill level, h, enters the equation just like labor-augmenting technology.

---

[1]This production function is also considered by Easterly, King, et al. (1994).

Capital, K, is accumulated by forgoing consumption, and the capital accumulation equation is standard:

$$\dot{K} = s_K Y - dK,$$

where s_K is the investment share of output (the rest going to consumption) and d is some constant exponential rate of depreciation greater than 0.

Our model differs from that in Chapter 3 in terms of the accumulation of skill h. There, an individual's skill level was simply a function of the amount of time the individual spent in school. Here, we generalize this idea as follows. "Skill" is now defined specifically as the range of intermediate goods that an individual has learned to use. As individuals progress from using hoes and oxen to using pesticides and tractors, the economy grows. Individuals learn to use more advanced capital goods according to

$$\dot{h} = \mu e^{\psi u} A^\gamma h^{1-\gamma}. \tag{6.4}$$

In this equation, u denotes the amount of time an individual spends accumulating skill instead of working. Empirically, we might think of u as years of schooling, although clearly individuals also learn skills outside of formal education. A denotes the world technology frontier. It is the index of the most advanced capital good invented to date. We assume $\mu > 0$ and $0 < \gamma \le 1$.[2]

Equation (6.4) has a number of features that merit discussion. First, notice that we preserve the basic exponential structure of skill accumulation. Spending additional time accumulating skill will increase the skill level proportionally. As in Chapter 3, this is intended to match the microeconomic evidence on returns to schooling. Second, the last two terms suggest that the change in skill is a (geometrically) weighted average of the frontier skill level, A, and the individual's skill level, h.

To see more clearly what equation (6.4) implies about skill accumulation, it can be rewritten by dividing both sides by h:

$$\frac{\dot{h}}{h} = \mu e^{\psi u} \left(\frac{A}{h}\right)^\gamma. \tag{6.5}$$

[2]Equation (6.4) is reminiscent of a relationship analyzed by Nelson and Phelps (1966) and more recently by Bils and Klenow (1996).

This equation makes clear the implicit assumption that it is harder to learn to use an intermediate good that is currently close to the frontier. The closer an individual's skill level, h, is to the frontier, A, the smaller the ratio A/h, and the slower his or her skill accumulation. This implies, for example, that it took much longer to learn to use computers thirty years ago, when they were very new, than it does today.

The technological frontier is assumed to evolve because of investment in research by the advanced economies in the world. Drawing on the results of the Romer model, we assume that the technology frontier expands at a constant rate, g:

$$\frac{\dot{A}}{A} = g.$$

A more complete model would allow individuals to choose to work in either the final-goods sector or in research, along the lines of Chapter 5. In a model like this, g would be a function of the parameters of the production function for ideas and the world rate of population growth. To simplify the analysis, however, we will not develop this more complete story. In this model, we assume that there is a world pool of ideas that are freely available to any country. In order to take advantage of these ideas, however, a country must first learn to use them.

6.2 STEADY-STATE ANALYSIS

As in earlier chapters, we will assume that the investment rate in the economy and the amount of time individuals spend accumulating skill instead of working are given exogenously and are constant. This is increasingly becoming an unpleasant assumption, and it is one we will explore in much greater detail in the next chapter. We also assume the labor force of the economy grows at the constant, exogenous rate n.

To solve for the balanced growth path in this economy, consider the skill accumulation equation in (6.5). Along a balanced growth path, the growth rate of h must be constant. Recall that since h enters the production function in equation (6.3) just like labor-augmenting technology, the growth rate of h will pin down the growth rate of output per worker, $y \equiv Y/L$, and capital per worker, $k \equiv K/L$, as well. From equation (6.5), we see that $\dot{h}/h$ will be constant if and only if A/h is constant, so that h and A must grow at the same rate. Therefore, we have

$$g_y = g_k = g_h = g_A = g, \qquad (6.6)$$

where as usual g_x denotes the growth rate of the variable x. The growth rate of the economy is given by the growth rate of human capital or skill, and this growth rate is tied down by the growth rate of the world technological frontier.

To solve for the level of income along this balanced growth path, we proceed in the usual fashion. The capital accumulation equation implies that along a balanced growth path the capital-output ratio is given by

$$\left(\frac{K}{Y}\right)^* = \frac{s_K}{n + g + d}.$$

Substituting this into the production function in equation (6.3) after rewriting it in terms of output per worker, we have

$$y^*(t) = \left(\frac{s_K}{n + g + d}\right)^{\alpha/1-\alpha} h^*(t), \qquad (6.7)$$

where the asterisk (*) is used to indicate variables along a balanced growth path. We have made explicit the fact that y and h are changing over time by including the t index.

Along the balanced growth path, the ratio of the skill level in our small economy to the most advanced capital good invented to date is pinned down by the accumulation equation for skill, equation (6.5). Using the fact that $g_h = g$, we know that

$$\left(\frac{h}{A}\right)^* = \left(\frac{\mu}{g}e^{\psi u}\right)^{1/\gamma}.$$

This equation tells us that the more time individuals spend accumulating skills, the closer the economy is to the technological frontier.[3]

Using this equation to substitute for h in equation (6.7), we can write output per worker along the balanced growth path as a function

[3] To be sure that the ratio h/A is less than one, we assume μ is sufficiently small.

of exogenous variables and parameters:

$$y^*(t) = \left(\frac{s_K}{n + g + d}\right)^{\alpha/1-\alpha} \left(\frac{\mu}{g}e^{\psi u}\right)^{1/\gamma} A^*(t). \qquad (6.8)$$

Equations (6.6) and (6.8) represent the key equations that describe the implications of our simple model for economic growth and development. Recall that equation (6.6) states that along a balanced growth path, output per worker increases at the rate of the skill level of the labor force. This growth rate is given by the growth rate of the technological frontier.

Equation (6.8) characterizes the level of output per worker along this balanced growth path. The careful reader will note the similarity between this equation and the solution of the neoclassical model in equation (3.8) of Chapter 3. The model developed in this chapter, emphasizing the importance of ideas and technology transfer, provides a "new growth theory" interpretation of the basic neoclassical growth model. Here, economies grow because they learn to use new ideas invented throughout the world.

Several other remarks concerning this equation are in order. First, the initial term in equation (6.8) is familiar from the original Solow model. This term says that economies that invest more in physical capital will be richer, and economies that have rapidly growing populations will be poorer.

The second term in equation (6.8) reflects the accumulation of skills. Economies that spend more time accumulating skills will be closer to the technological frontier and will be richer. Notice that this term is similar to the human capital term in our extension of the Solow model in Chapter 3. However, now we have made explicit what the accumulation of skill means. In this model, skills correspond to the ability to utilize more advanced capital goods. As in Chapter 3, the way skill accumulation affects the determination of output is consistent with microeconomic evidence on human capital accumulation.

Third, the last term of the equation is simply the world technological frontier. This is the term that generates the growth in output per worker over time. As in earlier chapters, the engine of growth in this model is technological change. The difference relative to Chapter 3 is that we now understand from the analysis of the Romer model where technological change comes from.

Fourth, the model proposes one answer to the question of why different economies have different levels of technology. Why is it that high-tech machinery and new fertilizers are used in producing agricultural products in the United States while agriculture in India or sub-Saharan Africa relies much more on labor-intensive techniques? The answer emphasized by this model is that the skill level of individuals in the United States is much higher than the skill level of individuals in developing countries. Individuals in developed countries have learned over the years to use very advanced capital goods, while individuals in developing countries have invested less time in learning to use these new technologies.

Implicit in this explanation is the assumption that technologies are available worldwide for anyone to use. At some level, this must be a valid assumption. Multinational corporations are always looking around the world for new places to invest, and this investment may well involve the use of advanced technologies. For example, cellular phone technology has proved very useful in an economy such as China's: instead of building the infrastructure associated with telephone lines and wires, several companies are vying to provide cellular communications. Multinational companies have signed contracts to build electric power grids and generators in a number of countries, including India and the Philippines. These examples suggest that technologies may be available to flow very quickly around the world, provided the economy has the infrastructure and training to use the new technologies.

By explaining differences in technology with differences in skill, this model cannot explain one of the empirical observations made in Chapter 3. There, we calculated total factor productivity (TFP) — the productivity of a country's inputs, including physical and human capital, taken together — and documented that TFP levels vary considerably across countries. This variation is not explained by the model at hand, in which all countries have the same level of total factor productivity. What then explains the differences? This is one of the questions we address in the next chapter.[4]

---

[4]Strictly speaking, we must be careful in applying the evidence from Chapter 3 to this model. For example, here the exponent $(1/\gamma)$ on time spent accumulating skills is an additional parameter.

6.3 TECHNOLOGY TRANSFER

In the model we have just outlined, technology transfer occurs because individuals in an economy learn to use more advanced capital goods. To simplify the model, we assumed that the designs for new capital goods were freely available to the intermediate-goods producers.

The transfer of technology is likely to be more complicated than this in practice. For example, one could imagine that the designs for new capital goods have to be altered slightly in different countries. The steering wheel on an automobile may need to be switched to the other side of the car, or the power source for an electrical device may need to be altered to conform to a different standard.

Technology transfer also raises the issue of international patent protection. Are intellectual property rights assigned in one country enforced in another? If so, then new designs may need to be licensed from the inventor before they can be used. As noted in Chapter 4, the ability to sell one's ideas in a global marketplace raises the returns to invention, thereby encouraging research.

Costs of adapting or licensing new designs are similar in some ways to the fixed costs of invention. Consider the case in which the inventor of our hypothetical WordTalk software program is deciding whether or not to produce a version of the software for China. Adapting the program to the Chinese language is somewhat like inventing an entirely new program. Substantial up-front development costs may be required to alter the program. The fact that China is a potentially enormous market may make these costs worth paying. But only, of course, if the intellectual property right is respected. In addition, the skills of the Chinese workforce are clearly relevant; it is not simply the number of people in China that matters, but the number of people who have computers and the skills to use them.[5]

---

[5]This setup is somewhat related to the idea of Basu and Weil (1996) that certain technologies may be appropriate only once a certain level of development has been reached. To use one of their examples, the latest maglev trains from Japan may not be useful in an economy such as that of Bangladesh, which depends on bicycles and bullock carts.

6.4 UNDERSTANDING DIFFERENCES IN GROWTH RATES

A key implication of equation (6.8) is that all countries share the same long-run growth rate, given by the rate at which the world technological frontier expands. In Chapters 2 and 3, we simply assumed this result. The simple model of technology transfer developed in this chapter provides one justification for this assumption.[6]

In models based on the diffusion of technology, the outcome that all countries share a common growth rate is typical. Belgium and Singapore do not grow solely or even mainly because of ideas invented by Belgians and Singaporeans. The populations of these economies are simply too small to produce a large number of ideas. Instead, these economies grow over time because they — to a greater or lesser extent — are successful at learning to use new technologies invented throughout the world. The eventual diffusion of technologies, even if it takes a very long time, prevents any economy from falling too far behind.[7]

How does this prediction that all countries have the same long-run growth rate match up with the empirical evidence? In particular, we know that average growth rates computed over two or three decades vary enormously across countries (see Chapter 1). While the U.S. economy grew at 1.4 percent, the Japanese economy grew at 5 percent per year from 1950 to 1990. Differences also exist over very long periods of time. For example, from 1870 to 1994, the United States grew at an average rate of 1.8 percent while the United Kingdom grew much more slowly at 1.3 percent. Doesn't the large variation in average growth rates that we observe empirically contradict this model?

The answer is no, and it is important to understand why. The reason is the one we have already discussed in Chapter 3. Even with no difference across countries in the long-run growth rate, we can explain the large variation in rates of growth with *transition dynamics*. To the extent

---

[6]The remainder of this section draws on Jones (1997a).

[7]One important exception is notable and will be discussed further in Chapter 7. Suppose that policies in an economy are so bad that individuals are not allowed to earn a return on their investments. This may prevent anyone from investing at all, which may result in a "development trap" in which the economy does not grow.

that countries are changing their position within the long-run income distribution, they can grow at different rates. Countries that are "below" their steady-state balanced growth paths should grow faster than *g*, and countries that are "above" their steady-state balanced growth paths should grow more slowly. What causes an economy to be away from its steady state? Any number of things. A shock to the country's capital stock (e.g., it is destroyed in a war) is a typical example. A policy reform that increases the investment in capital and skill accumulation is another.

This general point can be illustrated by taking a closer look at the behavior of the United States and the United Kingdom over the last 125 years. Figure 6.1 plots the log of GDP per capita in these two countries from 1870 to 1994. As noted above, growth in the United States over this period was fully a half-point higher than it was in the United Kingdom. However, a careful look at Figure 6.1 reveals that nearly all of this difference occurred before 1950, as the United States overtook

FIGURE 6.1 INCOME IN THE U.S. AND THE U.K., 1870–1994

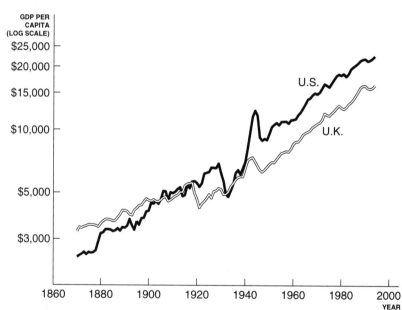

SOURCE: Maddison (1995).

the United Kingdom as the world's leading economy. From 1870 to 1950, the United States grew at 1.7 percent per year while the United Kingdom grew at only 0.9 percent. Since 1950, however, growth in these two economies has been nearly identical. The United States grew at 1.95 percent per year from 1950 to 1994 while the United Kingdom grew at 1.98 percent.

This example suggests that we have to be very careful in interpreting differences in average growth rates across economies. Even over very long periods of time they may differ. This is exactly what our model predicts. However, this does not mean that the underlying long-run growth rate varies across economies. The fact that Japan has grown much faster than the United States over the last forty years tells us very little about the underlying long-run growth rate of these economies. To infer that Japan will continue its astounding performance would be analogous to concluding in 1950 that growth in the United States would be permanently higher than growth in the United Kingdom. History has shown us that this second inference, at least, was incorrect.

The model in this chapter illustrates another important point. The principle of transition dynamics is not simply a feature of the capital accumulation equation in the neoclassical growth model, as was the case in Chapter 3. In this model, transition dynamics involve not only capital accumulation but also the technology transfer specification in equation (6.4). For example, suppose a country decides to reduce tariffs and trade barriers and open up its economy to the rest of the world. This policy reform might enhance the ability of the economy to transfer technologies from abroad; we can model this as an increase in μ. According to equation (6.8), a higher value of μ raises the economy's steady-state level of income. This means that at its current level, the economy is now below its steady-state income. What happens when this is the case? The principle of transition dynamics tells us that the economy grows rapidly as it transits to the higher income level.

EXERCISES

1. How might one pick a value of γ to be used in the empirical analysis of the model (as in Chapter 3)? Other things equal, use this value to discuss how differences in skills affect output per worker in the steady state, compared to the model used in Chapter 3.

2. This model explains differences in the level of income across countries by appealing to differences in s_K and u. What is unsatisfying about this explanation?

3. How does the model explain the differences in growth rates that we observe across countries?

4. What values of μ guarantee that h/A is less than 1?

5. This problem considers the effect on an economy's technological sophistication of an increase in the openness of the economy to technology transfer. Specifically, it looks at the short-run and long-run effects on h of an increase in μ. *Hint:* Look back at Figure 5.1 in Chapter 5.

   (a) Construct a graph with $\dot{h}/h$ on the vertical axis and A/h on the horizontal axis. In the graph, plot two lines:

   $$\frac{\dot{h}}{h} = \mu e^{\psi u} \left(\frac{A}{h} \right)$$

   and

   $$\dot{h}/h = g.$$

   (Note that we've assumed $\gamma = 1$.) What do these two lines mean, and what is the significance of the point where they intersect?

   (b) Starting from steady state, analyze the short-run and long-run effects of an increase in μ on the growth rate of h.

   (c) Plot the behavior of h/A over time.

   (d) Plot the behavior of $h(t)$ over time (on a graph with a log scale).

   (e) Discuss the consequences of an increase in openness to technology transfer on an economy's technological sophistication.

7
INFRASTRUCTURE AND LONG-RUN ECONOMIC PERFORMANCE

"It is often assumed that an economy of private enterprise has an automatic bias towards innovation, but this is not so. It has a bias only towards profit."
— Eric J. Hobsbawm (1969) cited by Baumol (1990), p. 893.

An important assumption maintained by all of the models considered up until now is that the investment rates and the time individuals spend accumulating skill are given exogenously. When we ask why some countries are rich while others are poor, our answer has been that rich countries invest more in capital and spend more time learning to use new technologies. However, this answer begs new questions: why is it that some countries invest more than others, and why do individuals in some countries spend more time learning to use new technologies?

Addressing these questions is currently one of the important subjects of research by economists who study growth and development, yet no consensus has emerged regarding the answer. As a result, there is no "canonical" model to help us outline an answer, as the Solow and Romer models did for earlier questions. Nevertheless, theory is such a useful way to organize one's thoughts that this chapter will present a very basic framework for thinking about these questions. The framework is motivated by a simple investment problem of the kind faced by business managers every day.[1]

---

[1] This chapter expands on a number of ideas presented by Hall and Jones (1996).

7.1 A BUSINESS INVESTMENT PROBLEM

Suppose you are the manager of a large, successful multinational corporation, and you are considering opening a subsidiary in a foreign country. How do you decide whether to undertake this investment?

One approach to evaluating this investment project is called *cost-benefit analysis*. In such an analysis, we calculate the total costs of the project and the total benefits, and if the benefits are larger, then we proceed.

Suppose that launching the business subsidiary involves a one-time setup cost F. For example, establishing the subsidiary may require obtaining both domestic and foreign business licenses, as well as business contacts with suppliers and distributors in the foreign country.

Once the business is set up, let's assume that it generates a profit every year that the business remains open. If Π denotes the expected present discounted value of the profit stream, then Π is the value of the business subsidiary once it has been set up. Why? Suppose that the parent company decides to sell the subsidiary after the one-time setup cost F has been paid. How much would another company be willing to pay to purchase the subsidiary? The answer is the present discounted value of the future profits, or at least what we expect them to be. This is exactly Π.

With this basic formalization of the investment problem, deciding whether or not to undertake the project is straightforward. If the value of the business after it is set up is larger than the cost of setting up the subsidiary, then the manager should undertake the investment project. The manager's decision is

$$\Pi \geq F \rightarrow \text{Invest}$$

$$\Pi < F \rightarrow \text{Do Not Invest}.$$

Although we have chosen a business project as the example to explain this analysis, the basic framework can be applied to the determination of domestic investment by a local business, the transfer of technology by a multinational corporation, or the decision to accumulate skills by an individual. The extension to technology transfer is inherent in the business example. A substantial amount of technology transfer presumably occurs in exactly this way — when multinational

corporations decide to set up a new kind of business in a foreign country. With respect to skill acquisition, a similar story applies. Individuals
must decide how much time to spend acquiring specific skills. For example, consider the decision of whether or not to spend another year
in school. F is the cost of schooling, both in terms of direct expendi-
tures and in terms of opportunity cost (individuals could spend the
time working instead of going to school). The benefit Π reflects the
present value of the increase in wages that results from the additional
skill acquisition.

What determines the magnitudes of F and Π in various economies
around the world? Is there sufficient variation in F and Π to explain
the enormous variation in investment rates, educational attainment,
and total factor productivity? The hypothesis we will pursue in this
chapter is that there is a great deal of variation in the costs of setting
up a business and in the ability of investors to reap returns from their
investments. Such variation arises in large part from differences in government policies and institutions — what we might call *infrastructure*.
A good government provides the institutions and infrastructure that
minimize F and maximize Π (or, more correctly, maximize $\Pi - F$),
thereby encouraging investment.

7.2 DETERMINANTS OF *F*

First, consider the cost of setting up a business subsidiary, F. Establishing a business, even once the *idea* driving the business has been
created — say the next "killer application" in computer software, or
even the notion that a particular location on a particular street would
be a great place to set up a hot-dog stand — requires a number of steps.
Each of these steps involves interacting with another party, and if that
party has the ability to "hold up" the business, problems can arise. For
example, in setting up a hot-dog stand, the property has to be purchased,
the hot-dog stand itself must be inspected by officials, and a business
permit may be necessary. Obtaining electricity may require another permit. Each of these steps offers an opportunity for a crafty bureaucrat to
seek a bribe or for the government to charge a licensing fee.

These kind of concerns can be serious. For example, after the land
and equipment have been purchased and several permits obtained, what

prevents the next bureaucrat — perhaps the one from whom the final license must be obtained — from asking for a bribe equal to Π (or slightly smaller)? At this point, the rational manager, with no choice other than canceling the project, may well be forced to give in and pay the bribe. All of the other fees and bribes that have been paid are "sunk costs" and do not enter the calculation of whether the next fee should be paid.

But, of course, the astute manager will envision this scenario from the very beginning, before any land or equipment is purchased and before any fees and bribes have been paid. The rational choice at this *ex ante* point is not to invest at all.

To residents of advanced countries like the United States or the United Kingdom, this issue may seem unimportant as a matter of practice. But this, as we will see, is exactly the point. Advanced countries provide a dynamic business environment, full of investment and entreprenuerial talent, exactly *because* such concerns are minimal.

There is a wealth of anecdotal evidence from other countries to suggest that this kind of problem can be quite serious. Consider the following example, which describes the problem of foreign investment in post-Communist Russia:

> To invest in a Russian company, a foreigner must bribe every agency involved in foreign investment, including the foreign investment office, the relevant industrial ministry, the finance ministry, the executive branch of the local government, the legislative branch, the central bank, the state property bureau, and so on. The obvious result is that foreigners do not invest in Russia. Such competing bureaucracies, each of which can stop a project from proceeding, hamper investment and growth around the world, but especially in countries with weak governments (Shleifer and Vishny 1993, pp. 615–16).

Another excellent example of the impact of government policies and institutions on the costs of setting up a business is provided by Hernando de Soto's *The Other Path* (1989). Like his more famous namesake, this contemporary de Soto gained renown by opposing the Peruvian establishment. What he sought, however, was not the riches of Peru, but rather the reason for the lack of riches in that country.[2]

---

[2]Long before exploring the Mississippi River and the southeastern United States, the more famous Hernando de Soto obtained his wealth as a Spanish conquistador of Peru.

In the summer of 1983, de Soto and a team of researchers started a small garment factory on the outskirts of Lima, Peru, for the express purpose of measuring the cost of complying with the regulations, red tape, and bureaucratic restrictions associated with a small entrepreneur starting a business. The researchers were confronted with 11 official requirements, such as obtaining a zoning certificate, registering with the tax authority, and procuring a municipal license. Meeting these official requirements took 289 person-days. Including the payment of 2 bribes (although 10 bribes were requested, "only" 2 were paid because they were absolutely required in order to continue the project), the cost of starting a small business was estimated to be the equivalent of 32 times the monthly minimum living wage.[3]

7.3 DETERMINANTS OF Π

Apart from the costs of setting up a business, what are the determinants of the expected profitability of the investment? We will classify these determinants into three categories: (1) the size of the market, (2) the extent to which the economy favors production instead of diversion, and (3) the stability of the economic environment.

The size of the market is one of the critical determinants of Π and therefore one of the critical factors in determining whether or not investments get undertaken. Consider, for example, the development of the Windows NT operating system by Microsoft. Would it have been worth the hundreds of millions of dollars required to develop this program if Microsoft could sell the software only in Washington state? Probably not. Even if every computer in Washington ran the Windows operating system, the revenue from sales of Windows NT would not cover development costs — there are simply too few computers in the state. In reality, the market for this software is, quite literally, the world, and the presence of a large market increases the potential reward for making the investment. This is another example of the "scale effect" associated with fixed or one-time costs.

This example suggests another point that is important: the relevant market for a particular investment need not be limited by national bor-

[3]See de Soto (1989).

ders. The extent to which an economy is open to international trade has a potentially profound influence on the size of the market. For example, building a factory to manufacture hard-disk drives in Singapore may not seem like a good idea if Singapore is the entire market; more people live in the San Francisco Bay area than in the entire country of Singapore. However, Singapore is a natural harbor along international shipping routes and has one of the world's most open economies. From Singapore, one can sell disk drives to the rest of the world.

A second important determinant of the profits to be earned on an investment is the extent to which the rules and institutions in an economy favor *production* or *diversion*. Production needs little explanation: an infrastructure that favors production encourages individuals to engage in the creation and transaction of goods and services. In contrast, diversion takes the form of the theft or expropriation of resources from productive units. Diversion may correspond to illegal activity, such as theft, corruption, or the payment of "protection money," or it may be legal, as in the case of confiscatory taxation by the government, frivolous litigation, or the lobbying of the government by special interests.

The first effect of diversion on a business is that it acts like a tax. Some fraction of the revenue or profits earned on an investment are taken away from the entrepreneur, detracting from the return on the investment. The second effect of diversion is that it encourages investment by the entrepreneur in finding ways to avoid the diversion. For example, the business may have to hire extra security guards or accountants and lawyers or pay bribes in order to avoid other forms of diversion. Of course, these investments in avoidance are also a form of diversion.

The extent to which the infrastructure of an economy favors production or diversion is primarily determined by the government. The government makes and enforces the laws that provide the framework for economic transactions in the economy. Moreover, in economies with infrastructures that favor diversion, the government is itself often a chief agent of diversion. Taxation is a form of diversion, and while some taxation is necessary in order for the government to be able to provide the rules and institutions associated with an infrastructure that favors production, the power to tax can be abused. Red tape and bureaucratic regulation enable government officials to use their influence to divert resources.

The power to make and enforce laws conveys an enormous power to the government to engage in diversion. This suggests the importance of an effective system of checks and balances and the separation of powers among several branches of government. This issue is reminiscent of the well-known aphorism "But who guards the guardians?" attributed to the Roman satirist Juvenal.[4]

Finally, the stability of the economic environment can itself be an important determinant of the returns to investing. An economy in which the rules and institutions are changing frequently may be a risky place in which to invest. Although the policies in place today may favor productive activities in an open economy, perhaps the policies tomorrow will not. Wars and revolutions in an economy are extreme forms of instability.

7.4 WHICH INVESTMENTS TO MAKE?

The infrastructure of an economy potentially has a large influence on investment. Economies in which the infrastructure encourages diversion instead of production will typically have less investment in capital, less foreign investment that might transfer technology, less investment by individuals in accumulating productive skills, and less investment by entrepreneurs in developing new ideas that improve the production possibilities of the economy.

In addition, the infrastructure of the economy may influence the type of investments that are undertaken. For example, in an economy in which theft is a serious problem, managers may invest capital in fences and security systems instead of productive machines and factories. Or in an economy in which government jobs provide the ability to earn rents by collecting taxes or bribes, individuals may invest in accumulating skills that allow them to obtain government employment instead of skills that would enhance production.

---

[4]Plato, another great writer about guardians, seems to think less of this problem in *The Republic*: "That they must abstain from intoxication has already been remarked by us; for of all persons, a guardian should be the last to get drunk and not know where he is. Yes, he said; that a guardian should require another guardian to take care of him is ridiculous indeed."

7.5 EMPIRICAL EVIDENCE

Our simple theoretical framework for analyzing investments has a number of general predictions. A country that attracts investments in the form of capital for businesses, technology transfer from abroad, and skills from individuals will be one in which

- the institutions and laws favor production over diversion,

- the economy is open to international trade and competition in the global marketplace, and

- the economic institutions are stable.

These characteristics encourage domestic investment by firms in physical capital (factories and machines), investment by foreign entrepreneurs that may involve the transfer of better technologies, and the accumulation of skills by individuals. Furthermore, such an environment encourages domestic entrepreneurship; individuals look for better ways to create, produce, or transport their goods and services instead of looking for more effective ways to divert resources from other agents in the economy.

What empirical evidence supports these claims? Ideally, one would like empirical measures of the attributes of an economy that encourage the various forms of investment. Then, one could look at the economies of the world to see if these attributes are associated with high rates of investment and successful economic performance.

Several measures of these attributes are available from a large research literature examining long-run economic performance. We will examine two of these measures here.[5] First, an index of "government anti-diversion policies" (GADP) is used to measure the extent to which the infrastructure of an economy favors production over diversion. This measure is assembled from a consulting firm that specializes in providing advice to multinational investors. Second, we use a measure of the extent to which economies are open to international trade: *openness*. The openness measure represents the percentage of years since 1950 for

---

[5]These measures are discussed in more detail in Hall and Jones (1996). Briefly, they are taken from Knack and Keefer (1995) and Sachs and Warner (1995).

which an economy is classified as open to international trade according to several objective criteria.

Figure 7.1 plots investment as a share of GDP for a number of countries against these determinants. To see how this figure is constructed, notice that it is a simple way of summarizing the data. We could have presented two plots: investment rates against GADP and investment rates against openness. To condense these two figures into one, we could have tried to present investment rates plotted against the sum of these two variables, GADP + openness. Instead, we present the investment rates plotted against a linear combination of these two variables, $b * \text{GADP} + c * \text{openness}$. To choose the weights b and c, we use a statistical procedure called "ordinary least squares" that produces the best "fit" of the investment data. The figure shows a strong relationship between these variables and investment: countries in which government policies strongly favor production over diversion and which are open

FIGURE 7.1   UNDERSTANDING DIFFERENCES IN INVESTMENT RATES

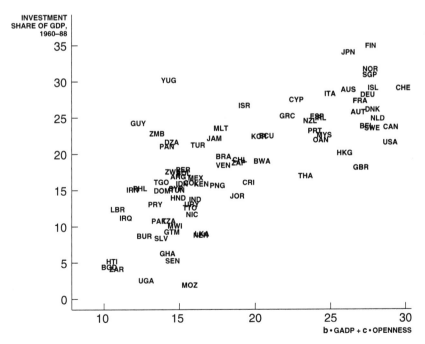

to international trade tend to have much higher investment as a share of GDP.

Figure 7.2 plots average years of schooling in each economy against GADP and openness.[6] Once again, a strong positive relationship between these variables is evident. Individuals invest much more of their time in accumulating skills in countries that are open to trade and favor production over diversionary activities.

This reasoning suggests a possible explanation of the stylized fact related to migration that we discussed in Chapter 1 (Fact 7). Recall that standard neoclassical theory suggests that rates of return are directly related to scarcity. If skilled labor is a scarce factor in developing economies, the return to skill in these economies should be high, and this should encourage the migration of skilled labor out of rich countries and

FIGURE 7.2 DIFFERENCES IN SKILL ACCUMULATION

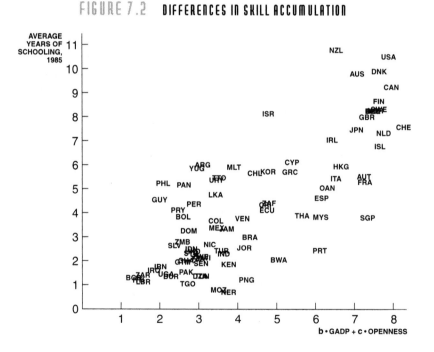

[6]The parameters used to weight GADP and openness (b and c) are not the same in Figures 7.1, 7.2, and 7.3. For each figure, the weights are chosen to generate the best fit of the data.

into poor countries. Empirically, however, the opposite pattern seems to occur. The explanation suggested here reverses this reasoning. Suppose that, at least to a first approximation, rates of return to skill are equalized by migration across countries. The stock of skills in developing countries is so low because skilled individuals are not allowed to earn the full return on their skills. Much of their skill is wasted by diversion — such as the payment of bribes and the risk that the fruits of their skill will be expropriated.[7]

Finally, Figure 7.3 plots the total factor productivity (TFP) level against GADP and openness. Recall from Chapter 3 that some countries get much more output from their inputs (capital and skills) than other countries. This is reflected in differences in TFP across countries. Fig-

FIGURE 7.3   DIFFERENCES IN TOTAL FACTOR PRODUCTIVITY

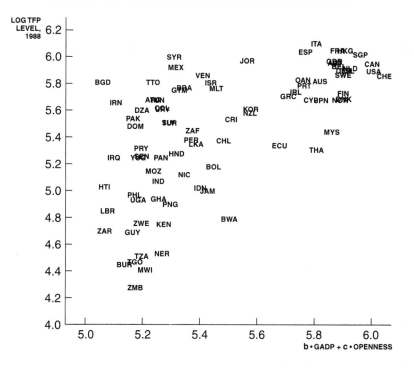

---

[7]Migration restrictions could then explain the observed pattern that skilled labor migrates from developing countries to developed countries when it has the opportunity.

ure 7.3 shows that these differences are also related to anti-diversion policies and openness to international trade. To see why this might be the case, consider a simple example in which individuals can choose to be either farmers or thieves. In the economy of Cornucopia, government policies strongly support production, no one is a thief, and society gets the maximum amount of output from its resources. On the other hand, in the economy of Kleptocopia, whose policies do not support production, thievery is an attractive alternative. Some individuals spend their time stealing from farmers. Thus some of the farmers' time that might have been spent farming must be used to guard the crops against thieves. Similarly some capital that might have been used for tractors is used for fences to keep out the thieves. The economy of Cornucopia gets much more output from its farmers and capital than does the economy of Kleptocopia. That is, Cornucopia has higher TFP.

This reasoning can help us rewrite the aggregate production function of an economy, like that used in Chapter 6 in equation (6.3), as

$$Y = IK^{\alpha}(hL)^{1-\alpha},$$

where I denotes the influence of an economy's infrastructure on the productivity of its inputs. With this modification, we now have a complete theory of production that accounts for the empirical results documented in Chapter 3. Economies grow over time because new capital goods are invented and the agents in the economy learn to use the new kinds of capital (captured by h). However, two economies with the same K, h, and L may still produce different amounts of output because the economic environments in which those inputs are used to produce output differ. In one, capital may be used for fences, security systems, and pirate ships, and skills may be devoted to defrauding investors or collecting bribes. In another, all inputs may be devoted to productive activities.

7.6 THE CHOICE OF INFRASTRUCTURE

Why is the infrastructure in some economies so much better than in others? Our questions about the determinants of long-run economic success are starting to resemble the beautiful *matrioshka* dolls of Russia, in which each figurine contains another inside it. Each of our answers to the question of what determines long-run economic success seems to raise another question.

This particular *matrioshka* is one that has greatly concerned economic historian and 1993 Nobel Prize winner Douglass North in much of his research. A principle that has served North well is that individuals in power will pursue actions that maximize their own utility. Far from leaders being "benevolent social planners" who seek to maximize the welfare of the individuals in society, government officials are self-interested, utility-maximizing agents just like the rest of us. In order to understand why certain laws, rules, and institutions are put in place in an economy, we need to understand what the governors and the governees have to gain and lose and how easy it is for the governees to replace the governor. Applying this reasoning to the broad sweep of economic history, North (1981) states,

> From the redistributive societies of ancient Egyptian dynasties through the slavery system of the Greek and Roman world to the medieval manor, there was a persistent tension between the ownership structure which maximized the rents to the ruler (and his group) and an efficient system that reduced transaction costs and encouraged economic growth. This fundamental dichotomy is the root cause of the failure of societies to experience sustained economic growth [p. 25].

This same argument can help us to understand what Joel Mokyr (1990, p. 209) calls the "greatest enigma in the history of technology": why China was unable to sustain its technological lead after the fourteenth century. For several hundred years during the Middle Ages and culminating in the fourteenth century, China was the most technologically advanced society in the world. Paper, the shoulder-collar for harnessing horses, moveable type for printing, the compass, the clock, gunpowder, ship-building, the spinning wheel, and iron casting were all invented in China centuries before they became known in the West. Yet by the sixteenth century many of these inventions had been either forgotten completely or simply left unimproved. It was the countries of western Europe rather than China that settled the New World and initiated the Industrial Revolution. Why? Historians disagree about the complete explanation, but a key factor is likely the lack of institutions supporting entrepreneurship.

What changed around the fourteenth century and led to the suppression of innovation and the demise of China's technological lead? One answer is the dynasty ruling China: the Ming dynasty replaced the Mongol dynasty in the year 1368. Mokyr, summarizing a plausible explanation advanced by several economic historians, writes,

> China was and remained an empire, under tight bureaucratic control. European-style wars between internal political units became rare in China after 960 A.D. The absence of political competition did not mean that technological progress could not take place, but it did mean that one decision maker could deal it a mortal blow. Interested and enlightened emperors encouraged technological progress, but the reactionary rulers of the later Ming period clearly preferred a stable and controllable environment. Innovators and purveyors of foreign ideas were regarded as troublemakers and were suppressed. Such rulers existed in Europe as well, but because no one controlled the entire continent, they did no more than switch the center of economic gravity from one area to another [p. 231].

7.7 GROWTH MIRACLES AND DISASTERS

The government policies and institutions that make up the infrastructure of an economy determine investment and productivity, and therefore also determine the wealth of nations. Fundamental changes in infrastructure can then generate growth miracles and growth disasters.

Two classic examples are Japan and Argentina. From 1870 until World War II, Japan's income remained around 25 percent of U.S. income. After the substantial reforms put in place at the end of the war, Japanese relative income rose sharply, far beyond recovery back to the 25 percent level. Today, as a result of this growth miracle, Japanese income is roughly two-thirds that of income in the United States. Argentina is a famous example of the reverse movement — a growth disaster. Argentina was as rich as most western European countries at the end of the nineteenth century, but by 1988 income per worker had fallen to only 42 percent of that of the United States. Much of this decline is attributable to disastrous policy "reforms," including those of the Juan Perón era.

Why do such fundamental changes in infrastructure occur? The answer probably lies in political economy and economic history. To predict when and whether such a change will occur in a particular economy surely requires detailed knowledge of the economy's circumstances and history. We can make progress by asking a slightly different question, however. Instead of considering the prospects for any individual economy, we can analyze the prospects for the world as a whole. Predicting the frequency with which such changes are likely to occur somewhere in the world is easier: we observe a large number of countries for several decades and can simply count the number of growth miracles and growth disasters.

A more formal way of conducting this exercise is presented in Table 7.1.[8] First, we sort countries into categories (or "bins") based on their 1960 level of GDP per worker relative to the world's leading economy (the United States during recent decades). For example, the bins correspond to countries with incomes of less than 5 percent of the world's leading economy, less than 10 percent but more than 5 percent, etc. Then, using annual data from 1960 to 1988 for 121 countries, we calculate the observed frequency with which countries move from one bin

TABLE 7.1 THE VERY-LONG-RUN DISTRIBUTION OF WORLD INCOME				
	Distribution			**Years to**
"Bin"	**1960**	**1988**	**Long-run**	**"shuffle"**
$\tilde{y} \leq .05$	15	17	8	307
$.05 < \tilde{y} \leq .10$	19	13	8	289
$.10 < \tilde{y} \leq .20$	26	17	11	194
$.20 < \tilde{y} \leq .40$	20	22	24	90
$.40 < \tilde{y} \leq .80$	17	22	30	199
$\tilde{y} > .80$	3	9	19	226

SOURCE: Jones (1997a).

Note: Entries under "Distribution" reflect the percentage of countries with relative incomes in each "bin." "Years to shuffle" indicates the number of years after which the best guess as to a country's location is given by the long-run distribution, provided that the country begins in a particular bin.

[8]This section is drawn from Jones (1997a). Quah (1993) first used this "Markov transition" approach to analyze the world income distribution.

to another. Finally, using these sample probabilities, we compute an estimate of the long-run distribution of incomes.[9]

Table 7.1 shows the distribution of countries across the bins in 1960 and 1988, as well as an estimate of the long-run distribution. The results are intriguing. The basic changes from 1960 to 1988 have been documented in Chapter 3. There has been some "convergence" toward the United States at the top of the income distribution, and this phenomenon is evident in the table. The long-run distribution, according to the results shown in the table, strongly suggests that this convergence will play a dominant role in the continuing evolution of the income distribution. For example, in 1960 only 3 percent of countries had more than 80 percent of U.S. income and only 20 percent had more than 40 percent of U.S. income. In the long run, according to the results, 19 percent of countries will have relative incomes of more than 80 percent of the world's leading economy and 49 percent will have relative incomes of more than 40 percent. Similar changes are seen at the bottom of the distribution: in 1988, 17 percent of countries had less than 5 percent of U.S. income; in the long run, only 8 percent of countries are predicted to be in this category.

Several comments on these results are worth considering. First, what is it in the data that delivers the result? The basic answer to this question is apparent in Figure 3.6 of Chapter 3. Looking back at this figure, one sees that there are more countries moving up in the distribution than moving down; there are more Italys than Venezuelas. In the last thirty years, we have seen more growth miracles than growth disasters.

Second, the world income distribution has been evolving for centuries. Why doesn't the long-run distribution look roughly like the current distribution? This is a very broad and important question. The fact that the data say that the long-run distribution is different from the current distribution indicates that something in the world continues to evolve: the frequency of growth miracles in the last thirty years must

---

[9]The sense in which this computation is different from that in Chapter 3 is worth emphasizing. There, we computed the steady state toward which each economy seems to be headed and examined the distribution of the steady states. Here, the exercise focuses much more on the very long run. In particular, according to the methods used to compute the long-run distribution in Table 7.1, if we wait long enough, there a is positive probability of any country ending up in any bin. This is discussed further in the coming examples.

have been higher than in the past, and there must have been fewer growth disasters.

One possible explanation of this result is that society is gradually discovering the kind of institutions and policies that are conducive to successful economic performance, and these discoveries are gradually diffusing around the world. To take one example, Adam Smith's *An Inquiry into the Nature and Causes of the Wealth of Nations* was not published until 1776. The continued evolution of the world income distribution could reflect the slow diffusion of capitalism during the last two hundred years. Consistent with this reasoning, the world's experiments with communism seem to be coming to an end only in the 1990s. Perhaps it is the diffusion of wealth-promoting institutions and infrastructure that accounts for the continued evolution of the world income distribution. Moreover, there is no reason to think that the institutions in place today are the best possible institutions. Institutions themselves are simply "ideas," and it is very likely that better ideas are out there waiting to be found. Over the broad course of history, better institutions have been discovered and gradually implemented. The continuation of this process at the rates observed during the last thirty years would lead to large improvements in the world income distribution.

The last column of Table 7.1 provides some insight regarding the length of time required to reach the long-run distribution. Consider shuffling a deck of playing cards right out of the pack, i.e., when they are initially sorted by suit and rank. How many shuffles does it take before the Ace of Spades has an equal probability of appearing anywhere in the deck? The answer turns out to be seven, provided the shuffles are perfect. Now suppose we consider a country in the richest income bin. How many years do we have to wait before the probability that the country is in a particular bin matches the probability implied by the long-run distribution? The last column of Table 7.1 reports that this number is 226 years. For a country starting from the poorest bin, it takes 307 years for initial conditions to cease to matter. The numbers are large, reflecting the fact that countries typically move very slowly through the world income distribution.

Other related experiments are informative. For example, one can calculate the frequency of "growth disasters." Although China was one of the most advanced countries in the world around the fourteenth century, today it has a GDP per worker of less than 7 percent that of the

United States. What is the likelihood of such a dramatic change? Taking a country in the richest bin, only after more than 125 years is there a 10-percent probability that the country will fall to a relative income of less than 10 percent.

What about growth miracles? The "Korean experience" is not all that unlikely. A country in the 10-percent bin will move to an income level in the 40-percent bin or higher with a 10-percent probability after 37 years. The same is true of the "Japanese experience": a country in the 20-percent bin will move to the richest category with a 10-percent probability after 50 years. Given that there are a large number of countries in these initial categories, one would expect to see several growth miracles at any point in time.

7.8 SUMMARY

The *infrastructure* of an economy — the rules and regulations and the institutions that enforce them — is a primary determinant of the extent to which individuals are willing to make the long-term investments in capital, skills, and technology that are associated with long-run economic success. Economies in which the government provides an environment that encourages production are extremely dynamic and successful. Those in which the government abuses its authority to engage in and permit diversion are correspondingly less successful.

Implicit in this theory of long-run economic performance is a theory that addresses the third fundamental question of economic growth discussed in the introduction of this book, the question of "growth miracles." How is it that some countries such as Singapore, Hong Kong, and Japan can move from being relatively poor to being relatively rich over a short span of time like forty years? Similarly, how is it that an economy like Argentina or Venezuela can make the reverse move?

This theory suggests that the answer is to be found in basic changes in the infrastructure of the economy: changes in the government policies and institutions that make up the economic environment of these economies.

Why do some economies develop infrastructures that are extremely supportive of production while others do not? Why was the Magna Carta written in England and why were its principles embraced throughout

Europe? How did England develop a separation of powers between the Crown and Parliament and a strong judicial system? Why did the United States benefit from the Constitution and the Bill of Rights? And most importantly, why, given historical experience, have some economies successfully adopted these institutions and the infrastructure associated with them while others have not? Fundamentally, these are the questions that must be addressed to understand the world pattern of economic success and how it changes over time.

EXERCISES

1. *Cost-benefit analysis.* Suppose an investment project yields a profit of $100 every year, starting one year after the investment takes place. Assume the interest rate for computing present values is 5 percent.

   (a) If $F = 1000, is the investment worth undertaking?

   (b) What if $F = 5000?

   (c) What is the cutoff value for F that just makes the investment worthwhile?

2. *Can differences in the utilization of factors of production explain differences in TFP?* Consider a production function of the form $Y = IK^\alpha(hL)^{1-\alpha}$, where I denotes total factor productivity and the other notation is standard. Suppose I varies by a factor of 10 across countries, and assume $\alpha = 1/3$.

   (a) Suppose differences in infrastructure across countries lead only to differences in the fraction of physical capital that is utilized in production (versus its use, say, as fences to protect against diversion). How much variation in the utilization of capital do we need in order to explain the variation in TFP?

   (b) Suppose both physical capital and skills vary because of utilization, and for simplicity suppose that they vary by the same factor. How much variation do we need now?

   (c) What do these calculations suggest about the ability of utilization by itself to explain differences in TFP? What else could be going on?

3. *Infrastructure and the investment rate.* Suppose that the marginal product of capital is equalized across countries because the world is an open economy, and suppose that all countries are on their balanced growth paths. Assume the production function looks like $Y = IK^\alpha L^{1-\alpha}$, where I reflects differences in infrastructure.

   (a) Show that differences in I across countries do not lead to differences in investment rates.

   (b) How might infrastructure in general still explain differences in investment rates?

4. Discuss the meaning of the quotation that began this chapter.

8 ALTERNATIVE THEORIES OF ENDOGENOUS GROWTH

I n this book, we have purposely limited ourselves to a few closely related models in an effort to formulate a general theory of growth and development. One result of this method of exposition is that we have not been able to discuss a large number of the growth models that have been developed in the last decade. This chapter presents a brief discussion of some of these other models.

The models described so far all have the implication that changes in government policies, such as subsidies to research or taxes on investment, have *level* effects but no long-run *growth* effects. That is, these policies raise the growth rate temporarily as the economy grows to a higher level of the balanced growth path. But in the long run, the growth rate returns to its initial level.

Originally, the phrase "endogenous growth" was used to refer to models in which changes in such policies could influence the growth rate permanently.[1] Differences in growth rates across countries were thought to reflect permanent differences in underlying growth rates. This is not the point of view presented in this book. Nevertheless, it is important to understand how these alternative models work. Developing such an understanding is the primary goal of this chapter. After we have presented the mechanisms at work, we will discuss some of the evidence for and against these models.

8.1 A SIMPLE ENDOGENOUS GROWTH MODEL: THE "AK" MODEL

One of the simplest models that allows for endogenous growth (in the sense that policies can influence the long-run growth rate) is easily derived by considering the original Solow model of Chapter 2. Consider our first exposition of that model in which there is no exogenous technological progress (i.e., $g \equiv \dot{A}/A = 0$). However, modify the production function so that $\alpha = 1$:

$$Y = AK, \tag{8.1}$$

where A is some positive constant.[2] It is this production function that gives the AK model its name.[3] Recall that capital is accumulated as individuals save and invest some of the output produced in the economy rather than consuming it:

$$\dot{K} = sY - dK, \tag{8.2}$$

where s is the investment rate and d is the rate of depreciation, both assumed to be constant. We assume that there is no population growth,

---

[1] According to *Merriam Webster's Collegiate Dictionary*, "endogenous" means "caused by factors inside the organism or system." Technological change is clearly endogenous in this sense in the models we have discussed in the later chapters of this book. However, without (exogenous) population growth, per capita income growth eventually stops. For this reason, models such as that presented in Chapter 5 are sometimes referred to as "semi-endogenous" growth models.

[2] The careful reader will notice that strictly speaking, with $\alpha = 1$, the production function in Chapter 2 should be written as $Y = K$. It is traditional in the model we are presenting to assume that output is *proportional* to the capital stock rather than exactly equal to the capital stock.

[3] Romer (1987) and Sergio Rebelo (1991) were early expositors of this model.

for simplicity, so that we can interpret upper-case letters as per capita variables (e.g., assume the economy is populated by only one person).

Now consider the familiar Solow diagram, drawn for this model in Figure 8.1. The dK line reflects the amount of investment that has to occur just to replace the depreciation of the capital stock. The sY curve is total investment as a function of the capital stock. Notice that because Y is linear in K, this curve is actually a straight line, a key property of the AK model. We assume that total investment is larger than total depreciation, as drawn.

Consider an economy that starts at point K_0. In this economy, because total investment is larger than depreciation, the capital stock grows. Over time, this growth continues: at every point to the right of K_0, total investment is larger than depreciation. Therefore, the capital stock is always growing, and growth in the model never stops.

The explanation for this perpetual growth is seen by comparing this figure to the original Solow diagram in Chapter 2. There, you will recall, capital accumulation was characterized by diminishing returns because $\alpha < 1$. Each new unit of capital that was added to the economy was slightly less productive than the previous unit. This meant that eventually total investment would fall to the level of depreciation, ending the

FIGURE 8.1   THE SOLOW DIAGRAM FOR THE AK MODEL

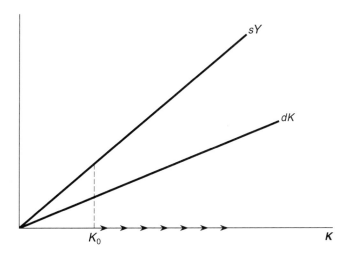

accumulation of capital (per worker). Here, however, there are *constant returns* to the accumulation of capital. The marginal product of each unit of capital is always A. It does not decline as additional capital is put in place.

This point can be shown mathematically, as well. Rewrite the capital accumulation equation (8.2) by dividing both sides by K:

$$\frac{\dot{K}}{K} = s\frac{Y}{K} - d.$$

Of course, from the production function in equation (8.1), $Y/K = A$, so that

$$\frac{\dot{K}}{K} = sA - d.$$

Finally, taking logs and derivatives of the production function, one sees that the growth rate of output is equal to the growth rate of capital, and therefore

$$g_Y \equiv \frac{\dot{Y}}{Y} = sA - d.$$

This simple algebra reveals a key result of the AK growth model: the growth rate of the economy is an increasing function of the investment rate. Therefore, government policies that increase the investment rate of this economy permanently will increase the growth rate of the economy permanently.

This result can be interpreted in the context of the Solow model with $\alpha < 1$. Recall that in this case, the sY line is a curve, and the steady state occurs when $sY = dK$ (since we have assumed $n = 0$). The parameter α measures the "curvature" of the sY curve: if α is small, then the curvature is rapid, and sY intersects dK at a "low" value of K^*. On the other hand, the larger α is, the further away the steady-state value, K^*, is from K_0. This implies that the transition to steady state is longer. The case of $\alpha = 1$ is the limiting case, in which the transition dynamics never end. In this way, the AK model generates growth endogenously. That is, we need not assume that anything in the model grows at some exogenous rate in order to generate per capita growth — certainly not technology, and not even population.

8.2 INTUITION AND OTHER GROWTH MODELS

The AK model generates endogenous growth because it involves a fundamental linearity in a differential equation. This can be seen by combining the production function and the capital accumulation equation of the standard Solow model (with the population normalized to one):

$$\dot{K} = sAK^\alpha - dK.$$

If $\alpha = 1$, then this equation is linear in K and the model generates growth that depends on s. If $\alpha < 1$, then the equation is "less than linear" in K, and there are diminishing returns to capital accumulation. If we divide both sides by K, we see that the growth rate of the capital stock declines as the economy accumulates more capital:

$$\frac{\dot{K}}{K} = sA\frac{1}{K^{1-\alpha}} - d.$$

Another example of how linearity is the key to growth can be seen by considering the exogenous growth rate of technology in the Solow model. Our standard assumption in that model can be written as

$$\dot{A} = gA.$$

This differential equation is linear in A, and permanent changes in g increase the growth rate permanently in the Solow model with exogenous technological progress. Of course, changes in government policies do not typically affect the exogenous parameter g, so we do not think of this model as generating endogenous growth. What these two examples show, however, is the close connection between linearity in a differential equation and growth.[4]

Other endogenous growth models can be created by exploiting this intuition. For example, another very famous model in this class is a model based on human capital, created by Robert E. Lucas, Jr., the 1995 Nobel laureate in economics. The Lucas (1988) model assumes a

---

[4]In fact, this intuition can be a little misleading in more complicated models. For example, in a model with two differential equations, one can be "less than linear" but if the other is "more than linear" then the model can still generate endogenous growth. See Mulligan and Sala-i-Martin (1993).

production function similar to the one we used in Chapter 3:

$$Y = K^{\alpha}(hL)^{1-\alpha},$$

where h is human capital per person. Lucas assumes that human capital evolves according to

$$\dot{h} = (1 - u)h,$$

where u is time spent working and $1-u$ is time spent accumulating skill. Rewriting this equation slightly, one sees that an increase in time spent accumulating human capital will increase the growth rate of human capital:

$$\frac{\dot{h}}{h} = 1 - u.$$

Notice that h enters the production function of this economy just like labor-augmenting technological change in the original Solow model of Chapter 2. So there is no need to solve this model further. It works just like the Solow model in which we call A human capital and let $g = 1 - u$. Therefore, in the Lucas model, a policy that leads to a permanent increase in the time individuals spend obtaining skills generates a permanent increase in the growth of output per worker.

8.3 EXTERNALITIES AND AK MODELS

We showed in Chapter 4 that the presence of ideas or technology in the production function means that production is characterized by increasing returns to scale. Then we argued that the presence of increasing returns to scale requires the introduction of imperfect competition: if capital and labor were paid their marginal products, as they would be in a world with perfect competition, no output would remain to compensate for the accumulation of knowledge.

There is an alternative way of dealing with the increasing returns that allows us to maintain perfect competition in the model. By the argument just given, individuals cannot be compensated for accumulating knowledge. However, if the accumulation of knowledge is itself an accidental by-product of other activity in the economy, it may still occur. That is, the accumulation of knowledge may occur because of an *externality*.

Consider a by-now-standard production function for an individual firm:

$$Y = BK^\alpha L^{1-\alpha}. \tag{8.3}$$

In this equation, there are constant returns to capital and labor. Hence, if B is accumulated endogenously, production is characterized by increasing returns.

Suppose that individual firms take the level of B as given. However, assume that in reality, the accumulation of capital generates new knowledge about production in the economy as a whole. In particular, suppose that

$$B = AK^{1-\alpha}, \tag{8.4}$$

where A is some constant. That is, an accidental by-product of the accumulation of capital by firms in the economy is the improvement of the technology that firms use to produce. An individual firm does not recognize this effect when it accumulates capital because it is small relative to the economy. This is the sense in which technological progress is *external* to the firm. Firms do not accumulate capital because they know it improves technology; they accumulate capital because it is a useful input into production. Capital is paid its private marginal product $\alpha Y/K$. However, it just so happens that the accumulation of capital provides an extraordinarily useful and unexpected benefit to the rest of the economy: it results in new knowledge.[5]

Combining equations (8.3) and (8.4), we obtain

$$Y = AKL^{1-\alpha}. \tag{8.5}$$

Assuming that the population of this economy is normalized to one, this is exactly the production function considered at the beginning of this chapter.

---

[5]This externality is sometimes called external "learning by doing." Firms learn better ways to produce as an accidental by-product of the production process. Kenneth Arrow, the 1972 Nobel Prize winner in economics, first formalized this process in a growth model (Arrow, 1962).

To summarize, there are two basic ways to deal with the increasing returns to scale that are required if one wishes to endogenize the accumulation of knowledge: imperfect competition and externalities. One can drop the assumption of perfect competition and model the accumulation of knowledge as resulting from the intentional efforts of researchers who search for new ideas. Alternatively, one can maintain perfect competition and assume that the accumulation of knowledge is an accidental by-product — an externality — of some other activity in the economy, such as capital accumulation.

As is evident from the order of presentation and the time spent developing each alternative, the opinion of this author is that knowledge accumulation is more accurately modeled as the desired outcome of entrepreneurial effort rather than as an accidental by-product of other activity. One need not observe for long the research efforts in Silicon Valley or the biotechnology firms of Route 128 in Boston to see the importance of the intentional search for knowledge. Some other evidence comparing these two approaches will be presented in the next section.

First however, it is worth noting that the externalities approach to handling increasing returns is sometimes appropriate, even in a model in which knowledge results from intentional R&D. Recall that in Chapter 5 we used imperfect competition to handle the increasing returns associated with the production of final output. However, we also used the externalities approach in handling a different production function, that for new knowledge. Consider a slight variation of the production function for knowledge in Chapter 5. In particular, let's rewrite equation (5.4) assuming $\lambda = 1$:

$$\dot{A} = \delta L_A A^\phi. \tag{8.6}$$

Externalities are likely to be very important in the research process. The knowledge created by researchers in the past may make research today much more effective; recall the famous quotation by Isaac Newton about standing on the shoulders of giants. This suggests that ϕ may be greater than 0.

Notice that with $\phi > 0$, the production function for new knowledge given in equation (8.6) exhibits increasing returns to scale. The return to labor is one, and the return to A is ϕ, for total returns to scale of $1 + \phi$. In Chapter 5, we treated A^ϕ as an externality. Individual researchers take A^ϕ as given when deciding how much research to perform, and they are not compensated for the "knowledge spillover" to future researchers that their research creates. This is simply an application of using the externalities approach to handle increasing returns.

8.4 EVALUATING ENDOGENOUS GROWTH MODELS

What this brief presentation of some alternative endogenous growth models shows is that it is relatively easy to write down models in which permanent changes in government policies generate permanent changes in growth rates for an economy. Of course, it is also easy to write down models in which this is not true, as we have done throughout this book. Which is a better way to think about economic growth? Do changes in government policies have permanent effects on the rate of economic growth?

At some level, the answer to this question must surely be "Yes." For example, we know that economic growth rates have increased in the last two hundred years relative to what they were for most of history. In Chapter 4, we presented the argument of a number of economic historians, such as Douglass North: this increase was due in large part to the establishment of property rights that allowed individuals to earn returns on their long-term investments.

However, this general feature of economic growth is predicted by models such as that in Chapter 5, where government policies in general do not affect the long-term growth rate. For instance, if we do not allow inventors to earn returns on their inventions (e.g., through a 100-percent tax), no one will invest and the economy will not grow.

The question, then, is more narrow. For example, if the government were to provide an additional 10-percent subsidy to research, education, or investment, would this have a permanent effect on the growth rate of the economy, or would it "only" have a level effect in the long run? Another way of asking this same question is the following: if the government were to provide an additional subsidy to research or investment, growth rates would rise for a while, according to many models. However, for how long would growth rates remain high? The answer could be 5 or 10 years, 50 or 100 years, or an infinite amount of time. This way of asking the question illustrates that the distinction between whether policy has permanent or transitory effects on growth is some-what misleading. We are really interested in how long the effects last.

One can use this reasoning as an argument in favor of models in which the effects are transitory. A very long transitory effect can come arbitrarily close to a permanent effect. However, the reverse is not true: a permanent effect cannot approximate an effect that lasts only for 5–10 years.

The recent literature on economic growth provides other reasons to prefer models in which changes in conventional government policies are modeled as having level effects instead of growth effects. The first reason is that there is virtually no evidence supporting the hypothe-sis that the relevant differential equations are "linear." For example, consider the simple AK model presented earlier in this chapter. This model requires us to believe the exponent on capital, α, is one. Recall that conventional estimates of the capital share using growth account-ing suggest that the capital share is about 1/3. If one tries to broaden the concept of capital to include human capital and externalities, one can raise the exponent to 2/3 or perhaps 4/5. However, there is very little evidence to suggest the coefficient is one.[6]

Another example can be seen in the research-based models of eco-nomic growth like those presented in Chapter 5. Recall that if the differ-ential equation governing the evolution of technology is linear, then the model predicts that an increase in the size of the economy (measured, for example, by the size of the labor force or the number or researchers) should increase per capita growth rates. For example, with $\lambda = 1$ and $\phi = 1$, the production function for ideas can be written

$$\frac{\dot{A}}{A} = \delta L_A.$$

Again, there is a great deal of empirical evidence that contradicts this prediction. Recall from Chapter 4 that the number of scientists and engineers engaged in research, a rough measure of L_A, has grown enor-mously over the last forty years. In contrast, growth rates have averaged about 1.8 percent for the entire time.[7] The evidence favors a model that is "less than linear" in the sense that $\phi < 1$.

---

[6] See, for example, Barro and Sala-i-Martin (1992) and Mankiw, Romer and Weil (1992).
[7] Jones (1995a) develops this argument in more detail.

Yet another example is found by considering more carefully the U.S. experience in the last century. There have been large movements in many variables that the endogenous growth literature highlights as important. For example, investment rates in education (measured, say, by the average educational attainment of each generation) have increased enormously over the past century. In 1940, for example, fewer than one out of four adults had completed high school; by 1995, however, more than 80 percent of adults had a high school diploma. Investment rates in equipment such as computers have increased greatly. Since 1950, the fraction of the labor force that consists of scientists and engineers engaged in formal R&D has increased by almost a factor of three. Despite these changes, average growth rates in the United States are no higher today than they were from 1870 to 1929 (recall Fact 5 in Chapter 1.)[8]

One final piece of evidence comes from observing differences across countries instead of differences over time within a country. A number of models in which policies can have growth effects predict that long-run growth rates should differ permanently across countries. The simple AK model and the Lucas model presented above, for example, share this prediction: differences in investment rates and differences in the rate at which individuals accumulate skills lead to permanent differences in growth rates. However, although growth rates vary substantially across countries, these differences are not always associated with differences in policies. Between 1960 and 1988, for example, the United States, Honduras, and Malawi all grew at roughly the same rate. The large differences in economic policies across these countries are reflected in levels of income, not growth rates.

8.5 WHAT IS ENDOGENOUS GROWTH?

It is fairly easy to construct models in which permanent changes in conventional government policies have permanent effects on an economy's long-run growth rate. However, the view in this book is that these models are not the best way to understand long-run growth. On the other hand, the development of these models and the empirical work

---

[8]This evidence is emphasized by Jones (1995b).

by economists to test and understand them have been tremendously useful in shaping our understanding of the growth process.

Long-run growth may not be endogenous in the sense that it can be easily manipulated at the whim of a policymaker. However, this is not to say that exogenous growth models like the Solow model provide the last word. Rather, we understand economic growth as the endogenous outcome of an economy in which profit-seeking individuals who are allowed to earn rents on the fruits of their labors search for newer and better ideas. The process of economic growth, in this sense, is clearly endogenous.

EXERCISES

1. Consider the AK model in which we do not normalize the size of the labor force to one.

   (a) Using the production function in equation (8.5) and the standard capital accumulation equation, show that the growth rate of output depends on L.

   (b) What happens if L is growing at some constant rate n?

   (c) Specify the form of the externality in equation (8.4) differently to avoid this implication.

   (d) Does labor affect production?

2. Does a permanent increase in s_K have a growth effect or a level effect in the Lucas model? Why?

3. Think about the market structure that underlies the Lucas model. Do we need perfect or imperfect competition? Do we need externalities? Discuss.

4. Historical evidence suggests that growth rates have increased over the very long run. For example, growth was slow and intermittent prior to the Industrial Revolution. Sustained growth became possible after the Industrial Revolution, with average growth rates of per capita income in the nineteenth century of approximately 1 percent per year. Finally, in the twentieth century, more rapid growth has emerged. Discuss this evidence and how it can be understood in

endogenous growth models (in which standard policies can affect long-run growth) and semi-endogenous growth models (in which standard policies have level effects in the long run).

5. What is the economic justification for thinking that the production function for new ideas takes the form given in equation (8.6)? In particular, why might this production function exhibit increasing returns to scale?

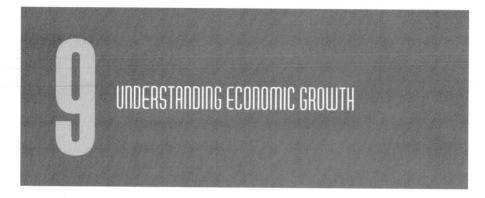

9 UNDERSTANDING ECONOMIC GROWTH

This book seeks to unravel one of the great mysteries of economics: How do we understand the enormous diversity of incomes and growth rates around the world? The typical worker in Ethiopia works a month and a half to earn what a U.S. or western European worker earns in a day. The typical worker in Japan has an income roughly 10 times that of his or her grandparents, while the typical worker in Australia, Chile, or the United States has only twice the income of his or her grandparents. With multinational corporations able to shift production across the world to minimize cost, and financial capital allocated through global markets, how do we explain these facts?

The questions we asked at the end of Chapter 1 organize the explanation:

- Why are we so rich and they so poor?

- What is the engine of economic growth?

- How do we understand growth miracles such as the rapid economic transformation of countries like Japan and Hong Kong?

The main points of this book are summarized by returning to these questions.

9.1 WHY ARE WE SO RICH AND THEY SO POOR?

Our first answer to this question is provided by the Solow model. Output per worker in steady state is determined by the rate of investment in private inputs such as physical capital and skills, by the growth rate of the labor force, and by the productivity of these inputs. Data on capital, education, and productivity strongly support the Solow hypothesis. Rich countries are those that invest a large fraction of their GDP and time in accumulating capital and skills. However, countries like the United States are rich not only because they have large quantities of capital and education per worker, but also because these inputs are used very productively. Not only are poor countries lacking in capital and education, but the productivity with which they use the inputs they possess is low as well.

The answer provided by the Solow framework raises additional questions. Why is it that some countries invest much less than others? Why are capital and skills used so much less productively in some locations? In Chapter 7, we showed the very important role played by an economy's laws, government policies, and institutions. This infrastructure shapes the economic environment in which individuals produce and transact. If the infrastructure of an economy encourages production and investment, the economy prospers. But if the infrastructure encourages diversion instead of production, the consequences can be detrimental. When entrepreneurs cannot be assured of earning a return on their investments, they will not invest. This is true for investments in capital, skills, or technology. Corruption, bribery, theft, and expropriation can dramatically reduce the incentives for investment in an economy, with devastating effects on income. Taxation, regulation, litigation, and lobbying are less extreme examples of diversion that affect investments of all kinds, even in advanced economies. Of course, advanced countries are advanced precisely because they have found ways to limit the extent of diversion in their economies.

9.2 WHAT IS THE ENGINE OF ECONOMIC GROWTH?

The engine of economic growth is invention. At a mathematical level, this is suggested by the Solow model: growth ceases in that model unless the technology of production improves exponentially. The Romer model, discussed in Chapters 4 and 5, examines this engine in great detail. Entrepreneurs, seeking the fame and fortune that reward invention, create the new ideas that drive technological progress.

Careful analysis of this engine reveals that ideas are different from most other economic goods. Ideas are nonrivalrous: my use of an idea (such as calculus, or the blueprint for a computer, or even the Romer model itself) does not preclude your simultaneous use of that idea. This property means that production necessarily involves increasing returns. The first copy of Windows NT required hundreds of millions of dollars to produce. But once the idea for Windows NT was created, the idea could be replicated essentially at no cost.

The presence of increasing returns to scale means that we cannot model the economics of ideas using perfect competition. Instead, we introduce imperfect competition into the model. Firms must be able to charge prices greater than marginal cost to cover the one-time expense required to create an idea. If Bill Gates had not expected to be able to charge more than the tiny marginal cost of Windows NT, he would not have invested hundreds of millions of dollars in creating the first copy. It is this wedge between price and marginal cost that provides the economic "fuel" for the engine of growth.

9.3 HOW DO WE UNDERSTAND GROWTH MIRACLES?

How do we understand the rapid economic transformation of economies like Hong Kong and Japan since World War II? Real incomes have grown at roughly 5 percent per year in these economies, compared to a growth rate of about 1.4 percent per year in the United States. The transformation associated with this rapid growth is nothing short of miraculous.

We understand growth miracles as reflecting the movement of an economy within the world income distribution. Something happened in the economies of Hong Kong and Japan to shift their steady-state relative incomes from values that were very low relative to the United

States to values that are relatively high. To make the transition from the low steady state to the high steady state, these economies must grow more rapidly than the United States. According to the principle of transition dynamics, the further a country is below its steady state, the faster the country will grow. Eventually, we expect the transition to the new steady state to be complete, and economic growth in Hong Kong and Japan to return to the growth rate given by the rate at which the world technological frontier expands. The fact that all growth miracles must come to an end doesn't make them any less miraculous. In the span of a few decades, the Japanese economy has been transformed from a relatively poor, war-weary economy into one of the leading economies of the world.

How does this tranformation take place? The answer is implicitly given by our explanation for the wealth of nations. If differences in infrastructure are a key determinant of differences in income across countries, then changes in infrastructure within an economy can lead to changes in income. Fundamental reforms that shift the incentives in an economy away from diversion and toward productive activities can stimulate investment, the accumulation of skills, the transfer of technologies, and the efficient use of these investments. By shifting the long-run steady state of an economy, such reforms engage the principle of transition dynamics and generate growth miracles.

9.4 CONCLUSION

Over the vast course of history, the process of economic growth was sporadic and inconsistent. Because institutions such as property rights were not sufficiently developed, discoveries and inventions were infrequent. The investments in capital and skills needed to generate and apply these inventions were absent. Similar problems impoverish many nations throughout the world today.

In recent centuries and in particular countries, the institutions and infrastructure that underlie economic growth have emerged. The result is that technological progress, the engine of growth, has roared to life. The consequences of this development for welfare are evident in the wealth of the world's richest nations. The promise implicit in our understanding of economic growth is that this same vitality merely lies dormant in the world's poorest regions.

APPENDIX A   MATHEMATICAL REVIEW

This appendix presents a simple review of the mathematical tools used throughout the book. It assumes some basic familiarity with calculus and covers techniques that are commonly used in modeling economic growth and development. A special effort has been made to include more words than equations. We hope this will permit a quick and easy understanding of the mathematics used in this book. For additional details, please refer to an introductory calculus textbook.

A.1 DERIVATIVES

The derivative of some function $f(x)$ with respect to x reveals how $f(\cdot)$ changes when x changes by a very small amount. If $f(\cdot)$ increases when x increases, then $df/dx > 0$, and vice versa. For example, if $f(x) = 5x$, then $df/dx = 5$, or $df = 5\,dx$: For every small change in x, $f(\cdot)$ changes by 5 times that amount.

A.1.1 WHAT DOES $\dot{x}$ MEAN?

In discussing economic growth, the most common derivative used is a derivative with respect to time. For example, the capital stock, K, is a function of time t, just like f was a function of x above. We can ask how the capital stock changes over time; this is fundamentally a question about the derivative dK/dt. If the capital stock is growing over time, then $dK/dt > 0$.

For derivatives with respect to time, it is conventional to use the "dot notation": dK/dt is then written as $\dot{K}$ — the two expressions are equivalent. For example, if $\dot{K} = 5$, then for each unit of time that passes, the capital stock increases by roughly 5 units. Why "roughly" instead of "exactly?" We will see in just a moment.

Notice that this derivative, $\dot{K}$, is very closely related to $K_{1997} - K_{1996}$. How does it differ? First, let's rewrite the change from 1996 to 1997 as $K_t - K_{t-1}$. This second expression is more general; we can evaluate it at $t = 1997$ or at $t = 1990$ or at $t = 1970$. Thus we can think of this change as a change per unit of time, where the unit of time is one period. Next, $\dot{K}$ is an *instantaneous* change rather than the change across an entire year. We could imagine calculating the change of the capital stock across one year, or across one quarter, or across one week, or across one day, or across one hour. *As the time interval across which we calculate the change shrinks, the expression $K_t - K_{t-1}$, expressed per unit of time, approaches the instantaneous change $\dot{K}$.* Formally, this is exactly the definition of a derivative. Let Δt be our time interval (a year, a day, or an hour). Then,

$$\lim_{\Delta t \to 0} \frac{K_t - K_{t-\Delta t}}{\Delta t} = \frac{dK}{dt}.$$

A.1.2   WHAT IS A GROWTH RATE?

Growth rates are used throughout economics, science, and finance. In economics, examples of growth rates include the inflation rate — if the inflation rate is 3 percent, then the price level is rising by 3 percent per year. The population growth rate is another example — population is increasing at something like 1 percent per year in the advanced economies of the world.

The easiest way to think about growth rates is as percentage changes. If the capital stock grew by 4 percent last year, then the change in the capital stock over the course of the last year was equal to 4 percent of its starting level. For example, if the capital stock began at $10 trillion and rose to $10.4 trillion, we might say that it grew by 4 percent. So one way of calculating a growth rate is as a percentage change:

$$\frac{K_t - K_{t-1}}{K_{t-1}}.$$

For mathematical reasons that we will explore below, it turns out to be easier in much of economics to think about the *instantaneous* growth rate. That is, we define the growth rate to be the derivative dK/dt divided by its starting value, K. As discussed in the preceding section, we use $\dot{K}$ to represent dK/dt. Therefore, $\dot{K}/K$ is a growth rate. Whenever you see such a term, just think *"percentage change."*

A few examples may help clarify this concept. First, suppose $\dot{K}/K =$ .05; this says that the capital stock is growing at 5 percent per year. Second, suppose $\dot{L}/L = .01$; this says that the labor force is growing at 1 percent per year.

8.1.3 GROWTH RATES AND NATURAL LOGS

The mathematical reason why this definition of growth rates is convenient can be seen by considering several properties of the natural logarithm:

1. If $z = xy$, then $\log z = \log x + \log y$.

2. If $z = x/y$, then $\log z = \log x - \log y$.

3. If $z = x^\beta$, then $\log z = \beta \log x$.

4. If $y = f(x) = \log x$, then $dy/dx = 1/x$.

5. If $y(t) = \log x(t)$, then

$$\frac{dy}{dt} = \frac{dy}{dx}\frac{dx}{dt} = \frac{1}{x}\dot{x} = \frac{\dot{x}}{x}.$$

The first of these properties is that the natural log of the product of two (or more) variables is the sum of the logs of the variables. The second property is very similar, but relates the division of two variables to the difference of the logs. The third property allows us to convert exponents into multiplicative terms. The fourth property says that the derivative of the log of some variable x is just $1/x$.

The fifth property is a key one. In effect, it says that *the derivative with respect to time of the log of some variable is the growth rate of that variable.* For example, consider the capital stock, K. According to property 5 above,

$$\frac{d \log K}{dt} = \frac{\dot{K}}{K},$$

which, as we saw in Section A.1.3, is the growth rate of K.

A.1.4 "TAKE LOGS AND DERIVATIVES"

Each of the properties of the natural logarithm listed in the preceding section is used in the "take logs and derivatives" example below. Consider a simple Cobb-Douglas production function:

$$Y = K^\alpha L^{1-\alpha}.$$

If we take logs of both sides,

$$\log Y = \log K^\alpha + \log L^{1-\alpha}.$$

Moreover, by property 3 discussed in section A.1.3,

$$\log Y = \alpha \log K + (1 - \alpha) \log L.$$

Finally, by taking derivatives of both sides with respect to time, we can see how the growth rate of output is related to the growth rate of the inputs in this example:

$$\frac{d \log Y}{dt} = \alpha \frac{d \log K}{dt} + (1 - \alpha) \frac{d \log L}{dt},$$

which implies that

$$\frac{\dot{Y}}{Y} = \alpha \frac{\dot{K}}{K} + (1 - \alpha) \frac{\dot{L}}{L}.$$

This last equation says that the growth rate of output is a weighted average of the growth rates of capital and labor.

A.1.5 RATIOS AND GROWTH RATES

Another very useful application of these properties is in situations in which the ratio of two variables is constant. First, notice that if a variable is constant, its growth rate is zero — it is not changing, so its time derivative is zero.

Now, suppose that $z = x/y$ and suppose we know that z is constant over time, i.e., $\dot{z} = 0$. Taking logs and derivatives of this relationship, one can see that

$$\frac{\dot{z}}{z} = \frac{\dot{x}}{x} - \frac{\dot{y}}{y} = 0 \implies \frac{\dot{x}}{x} = \frac{\dot{y}}{y}.$$

Therefore, if the ratio of two variables is constant, the growth rates of those two variables must be the same. Intuitively, this makes sense. If the numerator of the ratio were growing faster than the denominator, the ratio itself would have to be growing over time.

A.1.6 △LOG VERSUS PERCENTAGE CHANGE

Suppose a variable exhibits exponential growth:

$$y(t) = y_0 e^{gt}.$$

For example, $y(t)$ could measure per capita output for an economy. Then,

$$\log y(t) = \log y_0 + gt,$$

and therefore the growth rate, g, can be calculated as

$$g = \frac{1}{t}(\log y(t) - \log y_0).$$

Or, calculating the growth rate between time t and time $t - 1$,

$$g = \log y(t) - \log y(t - 1) \equiv \Delta \log y(t).$$

These last two equations provide the justification for calculating growth rates as the change in the log of a variable.

How does this calculation relate to the more familiar percentage change? The answer is straightforward:

$$\frac{y(t) - y(t - 1)}{y(t - 1)} = \frac{y(t)}{y(t - 1)} - 1$$

$$= e^g - 1.$$

Recall that the Taylor approximation for the exponential function is $e^x \approx 1 + x$ for small values of x. Applying this to the last equation shows that the percentage change and the change in log calculations are approximately equivalent for small growth rates:

$$\frac{y(t) - y(t-1)}{y(t-1)} \approx g.$$

A.2 INTEGRATION

Integration is the calculus equivalent of summation. For example, one could imagine a production function written as

$$Y = \sum_{i=1}^{10} x_i = x_1 + x_2 + \cdots + x_{10}, \tag{A.1}$$

that is, output is simply the sum of ten different inputs. One could also imagine a related production function

$$Y = \int_0^{10} x_i \, di. \tag{A.2}$$

In this production function, output is the weighted sum of a continuum of inputs x_i that are indexed by the interval of the real line between 0 and 10. Obviously, there are an infinite number of inputs in this second production function, because there are an infinite number of real numbers in this interval. However, each input is "weighted" by the average size of an interval, di, which is very small. This keeps production finite, even if each of our infinite number of inputs is used in positive amounts. Don't get too confused by this reasoning. Instead, think of integrals as sums, and think of the second production function in the same way that you would think of the first. To show you that you won't go too far wrong, suppose that 100 units of each input is used in both cases: $x_i = 100$ for all i. Output with the production function in equation (A.1) is then equal to 1,000. What is output with the production function in equation (A.2)?

$$Y = \int_0^{10} 100 \, di = 100 \int_0^{10} di = 1,000.$$

Output is the same in both cases.

A.2.1 AN IMPORTANT RULE OF INTEGRATION

In this last step we used an important rule of integration: Integrals and derivatives are like multiplication and division — they "cancel":

$$\int dx = x + C,$$

where C is some constant, and

$$\int_a^b dx = b - a.$$

A.3 SIMPLE DIFFERENTIAL EQUATIONS

There is really only one differential equation in this book that we ever need to solve: the key differential equation that relates growth rates and levels. Its solution is straightforward.

Suppose a variable x is growing at some constant rate g. That is,

$$\frac{\dot{x}}{x} = g.$$

What does this imply about the level of x? The answer can be seen by noting that the growth rate of x is the derivative of the log:

$$\frac{d \log x}{dt} = g.$$

The key to solving this differential equation is to recall that to "undo" derivatives, we use integrals. First, rewrite the differential equation slightly:

$$d \log x = g \, dt.$$

Now, integrate both sides of this equation:

$$\int d \log x = \int g \, dt,$$

which implies that

$$\log x = gt + C,$$

where, once again, C is some constant. Therefore, a variable that is growing at a constant rate is a linear function of time. Taking the exponential of both sides, we get

$$x = \overline{C}e^{gt}, \tag{A.3}$$

where $\overline{C}$ is another constant.[1] To figure out what the constant is, set $t = 0$ to see that $x(0) = \overline{C}$. Typically, we assume that $x(0) = x_0$, that is, at time 0, x takes on a certain value x_0. This is known as an *initial condition*. Thus $\overline{C} = x_0$. This reasoning shows why we say that a variable growing at a constant rate exhibits "exponential" growth. Figure A.1 plots $x(t)$ for $x_0 = 1$ and $g = .05$.

It is often convenient to plot variables that are growing at an exponential rate in log terms. That is, instead of plotting $x(t)$, we plot $\log x(t)$. To see why, notice that for the example we have just considered, $\log x(t)$

FIGURE A.1   EXPONENTIAL GROWTH

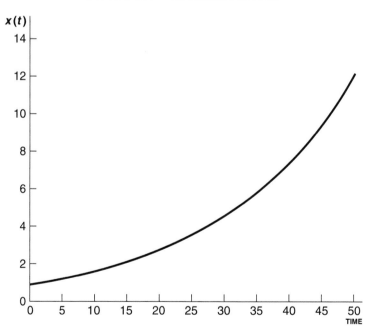

---

[1] To be exact, $\overline{C} = e^C$.

is a linear function of time:

$$\log x(t) = \log x_0 + gt.$$

Figure A.2 plots $\log x(t)$ to show this linear relationship. Note that the slope of the relationship is the growth rate of $x(t)$, $g = .05$.

Finally, notice that it is sometimes convenient to plot the log of a variable but then to change the labels of the graph. For example, we might plot the log of GDP per capita in the U.S. economy over the last 125 years, as in Figure 1.3 in Chapter 1, to illustrate the fact that the average growth rate is fairly constant. Per capita income in 1994 was nearly $25,000. The log of 25,000 is 10.13, which is not a very informative label. Therefore, we plot the log of GDP per capita, and then relabel the point 10.13 as $25,000. Similarly, we relabel the point 8.52 as $5,000. (Why?) This relabeling is typically indicated by the statement that the variable is plotted on a "log scale."

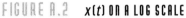 FIGURE A.2   *x(t)* ON A LOG SCALE

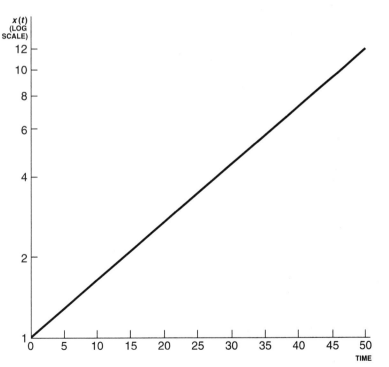

A.3.1 COMPOUND INTEREST

A classic example to illustrate the difference between the "instanta-neous" growth rates used in this book and the "percentage change" calculations that we are all familiar with is the difference between *continuously* compounded interest and interest that is compounded daily or yearly. Recall that interest is compounded when a bank pays you interest on your interest. (This contrasts with simple interest, where a bank pays interest only on the principal.) Suppose that you open a banking account with $100 and the bank pays you an interest rate of 5 percent compounded yearly. Let $x(t)$ be the bank balance, and let t indicate the number of years the $100 has been in the bank. Then, for interest compounded yearly at 5 percent, $x(t)$ behaves according to

$$x(t) = 100(1 + .05)^t.$$

The first column of Table A.1 reports the bank balance at various points in time.

Now suppose instead of being compounded yearly the interest is compounded continously — it is not compounded every year, or every day, or every minute, but rather it is compounded every instant. As in the case of interest compounded yearly, the bank balance is growing at a rate of 5 percent. However, now that growth rate is an *instantaneous* growth rate instead of an *annual* growth rate. In this case, the bank

TABLE A.1 BANK BALANCE WITH COMPOUND INTEREST AT 5 PERCENT		
Years	Compounded yearly	Compounded continuously
0	$100.0	$100.0
1	105.0	105.1
2	110.2	110.5
5	127.6	128.4
10	162.9	164.9
14	198.0	201.4
25	338.6	349.0

balance obeys the differential equation $\dot{x}/x = .05$, and from the calculations we have done before leading us to equation (A.3), we know the solution to this differential equation is

$$x(t) = 100e^{.05t}.$$

The second column of Table A.1 reports the bank balance for this case. Notice that even after one year, the continuous compounding produces a balance slightly larger than $105, but the differences are fairly small (at least for the first fifteen years or so).[2]

This example comparing continuously compounded interest with annually compounded interest is mathematically equivalent to comparing instantaneous growth rates of, say, output per worker to annual percentage changes in output per worker.

A.4 MAXIMIZATION OF A FUNCTION

Many problems in economics take the form of *optimization* problems: a firm maximizes profits, consumers maximize utility, etc. Mathematically, these optimization problems are solved by finding the *first-order conditions* for the problem.

For an optimization problem with only one choice variable and no constraints, the solution is particularly easy. Consider the following problem:

$$\max_{x} f(x).$$

The solution is usually found from the first-order condition that $f'(x) = 0$. Why? Suppose we guess a value x_1 for the solution and $f'(x_1) > 0$. Obviously, then, we could increase x slightly and this would increase the function. So x_1 cannot be a solution. A similar trick would work if $f'(x_1) < 0$. Therefore, the first-order condition is that the derivative, $f'(x)$, equal exactly zero at the solution.

How do we know if some point x^* that satisfies $f'(x^*) = 0$ is a maximum or a minimum (or an inflection point)? The answer involves

---

[2]Notice also that the $100 doubles in about fourteen years if the interest rate is 5 percent, as predicted by the formula in Chapter 1.

the *second-order condition*. Figure A.3 provides the intuition behind the second-order condition. For x^* to be a maximum, it must be the case that $f''(x^*) < 0$. That is, the first derivative must be decreasing in x at the point x^*. This way, $f'(x)$ is positive at a point just below x^* and negative at a point just above x^*. That is, $f(\cdot)$ is increasing at points below x^* and decreasing at points above x^*.

More general optimization problems with more variables and constraints follow this same kind of reasoning. For example, suppose a firm takes the wage w, the rental rate r, and the price p of its output as given and has to decide how much capital K and labor L to hire in order to produce some output:

$$\max_{K,L} \pi = pF(K, L) - wL - rK.$$

The first-order conditions for this problem are the familiar conditions that the wage and rental rates equal the marginal revenue product of labor and capital:

$$p\frac{\partial F}{\partial L} = w$$

FIGURE A.3   MAXIMIZING A FUNCTION

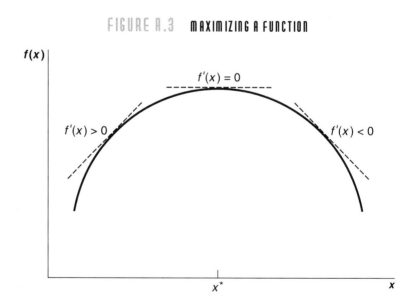

and

$$p\frac{\partial F}{\partial K} = r.$$

The second-order conditions for a problem with more than one choice variable are a bit more complicated, and we will simply assume that the second-order conditions hold throughout this book (the problems are set up so that this is a valid assumption). Problems with constraints are only a bit more complicated. Refer to an intermediate microeconomics textbook for the techniques of constrained optimization. These techniques will not be used in this book.

EXERCISES

1. Suppose $x(t) = e^{.05t}$ and $z(t) = e^{.01t}$. Calculate the growth rate of $y(t)$ for each of the following cases:

   (a) $y = x$

   (b) $y = z$

   (c) $y = xz$

   (d) $y = x/z$

   (e) $y = x^\beta z^{1-\beta}$, where $\beta = 1/2$

   (f) $y = (x/z)^\beta$, where $\beta = 1/3$.

2. Express the growth rate of y in terms of the growth rates of k, l, and m for the following cases. Assume β is some arbitrary constant.

   (a) $y = k^\beta$

   (b) $y = k/m$

   (c) $y = (klm)^\beta$

   (d) $y = (kl)^\beta (1/m)^{1-\beta}$.

3. Assume $\dot{x}/x = .10$ and $\dot{z}/z = .02$, and suppose that $x(0) = 2$ and $z(0) = 1$. Calculate the numerical values of $y(t)$ for $t = 0, t = 1, t = 2,$ and $t = 10$ for the following cases:

(a) $y = xz$

(b) $y = z/x$

(c) $y = x^\beta z^{1-\beta}$, where $\beta = 1/3$.

4. Using the data from Appendix B, pp. 180–83, on GDP per worker in 1960 and 1990, calculate the average annual growth rate of GDP per worker for the following countries: the United States, Canada, Argentina, Chad, Brazil, Thailand. Confirm that this matches the growth rates reported in Appendix B.

5. Assuming population growth and labor force growth are the same (why wouldn't they be?), use the results from the previous exercise together with the population growth rates from Appendix B to calculate the average annual growth rate of GDP for the same group of countries.

APPENDIX B   DATA ON ECONOMIC GROWTH

With the explosion of the World Wide Web in recent years, much of the data that economists analyze in studying economic growth is now available on-line. At the time of this writing (summer 1997), some of the most useful Web sites related to growth are

- Bill Goffe's Resources for Economists on the Internet

    http://econwpa.wustl.edu/EconFAQ/EconFAQ.html

- Summers-Heston Penn World Tables

    http://cansim.epas.utoronto.ca:5680/pwt/index.html

- World Bank Economic Growth Project

    http://www.worldbank.org/html/prdmg/grthweb/growth_t.htm

- World Bank Social Indicators of Development

    http://www.ciesin.org/IC/wbank/sid-home.html

- CIA World Factbook 1996

    http://www.odci.gov/cia/publications/pubs.html

- Nuffield College, Oxford, Growth Page

    http://www.nuff.ox.ac.uk/Economics/Growth/

As with most things related to the Internet, this list will almost surely be out of date by the time it is read. However, the first site listed is a

TABLE B.1	DEFINITIONS
$\hat{y}$	GDP per worker, relative to the U.S.
$g(60, 90)$	Average annual growth rate of GDP per worker, 1960–90
s_K	Average investment share of GDP, 1980–90
u	Average educational attainment in years, 1985
n	Average population growth rate, 1980–90
—	Data not available

Note: U.S. GDP per worker in 1990 was $36,810, and in 1960 was $24,465.

well-maintained collection of links to resources for economists. All of the remaining sites should be listed there.

The remainder of this appendix focuses on two tables. These tables report a number of key statistics for 104 countries. Table B.1 contains definitions, and Table B.2 contains the actual data. All of the data except for the educational attainment variable are taken from the Penn World Tables, Mark 5.6. An earlier version of this data is discussed by Summers and Heston (1991). The educational attainment variable was constructed by Barro and Lee (1993).

				TABLE B.2	COUNTRY DATA			
Country	**Code**	**$\hat{y}_{90}$**	**$\hat{y}_{60}$**	**$g(60, 90)$**	**s_K**	**u**	**n**
Luxembourg	LUX	1.03	.77	.023	.267	—	.005
U.S.A.	USA	1.00	1.00	.014	.210	11.8	.009
Canada	CAN	.93	.79	.019	.253	10.4	.010
Switzerland	CHE	.89	.82	.016	.306	9.1	.006
Belgium	BEL	.86	.58	.027	.207	9.2	.001
Netherlands	NLD	.85	.70	.020	.210	8.6	.006
Italy	ITA	.84	.45	.034	.244	6.3	.002
France	FRA	.82	.55	.027	.252	6.5	.005
Australia	AUS	.82	.78	.015	.269	10.2	.015
West Germany	DEU	.80	.57	.025	.245	8.5	.003

(*continued*)

TABLE B.2   (CONTINUED)

Country	Code	$\hat{y}_{90}$	$\hat{y}_{60}$	$g(60, 90)$	s_K	u	n
Norway	NOR	.80	.58	.024	.276	10.4	.004
Sweden	SWE	.77	.71	.016	.212	9.4	.003
Finland	FIN	.74	.47	.029	.320	9.5	.004
U.K.	GBR	.73	.60	.020	.171	8.7	.002
Austria	AUT	.73	.44	.030	.247	6.6	.002
Spain	ESP	.72	.34	.039	.239	5.6	.004
New Zealand	NZL	.69	.87	.006	.241	12.0	.008
Iceland	ISL	.68	.52	.023	.249	7.9	.011
Denmark	DNK	.68	.60	.018	.215	10.3	.000
Singapore	SGP	.66	.20	.053	.361	4.5	.017
Ireland	IRL	.65	.34	.035	.238	8.0	.003
Israel	ISR	.65	.39	.030	.196	9.4	.018
Hong Kong	HKG	.62	.17	.057	.195	7.5	.012
Japan	JPN	.61	.20	.050	.338	8.5	.006
Trinidad/Tobago	TTO	.54	.69	.005	.137	6.5	.013
Taiwan	OAN	.50	.14	.057	.237	7.0	.013
Cyprus	CYP	.49	.21	.042	.253	7.1	.011
Greece	GRC	.48	.21	.041	.199	6.7	.005
Venezuela	VEN	.47	.83	−.005	.154	5.4	.026
Mexico	MEX	.46	.39	.019	.160	4.4	.020
Portugal	PRT	.45	.20	.041	.207	3.8	.001
South Korea	KOR	.43	.11	.060	.299	7.8	.012
Syria	SYR	.43	.23	.034	.149	4.0	.033
Argentina	ARG	.36	.47	.005	.146	6.7	.014
Jordan	JOR	.34	.18	.035	.164	4.3	.041
Malaysia	MYS	.34	.17	.037	.282	5.4	.026
Algeria	DZA	.33	.26	.021	.236	2.4	.029
Chile	CHL	.32	.36	.010	.210	6.5	.017
Uruguay	URY	.32	.40	.006	.136	6.5	.006
Fiji	FJI	.32	.31	.015	.152	6.8	.014
Iran	IRN	.31	.42	.004	.191	3.3	.035
Brazil	BRA	.30	.23	.023	.169	3.5	.021
Mauritius	MUS	.28	.24	.018	.096	4.6	.011

(*continued*)

Country	Code	$\hat{y}_{90}$	$\hat{y}_{60}$	$g(60, 90)$	s_K	u	n
Colombia	COL	.27	.22	.020	.155	4.5	.020
Yugoslavia	YUG	.27	.18	.028	.301	7.2	.007
Costa Rica	CRI	.27	.28	.013	.169	5.3	.027
South Africa	ZAF	.26	.26	.014	.170	5.0	.025
Namibia	NAM	.26	.20	.023	.115	—	.030
Seychelles	SYC	.25	.10	.043	.180	—	.008
Ecuador	ECU	.25	.18	.024	.195	5.6	.026
Tunisia	TUN	.24	.16	.027	.123	2.5	.023
Turkey	TUR	.23	.13	.033	.221	3.3	.023
Gabon	GAB	.22	.14	.028	.228	—	.035
Panama	PAN	.22	.19	.018	.157	6.3	.021
Czechoslovakia	CSK	.21	.14	.028	.273	—	.003
Guatemala	GTM	.20	.22	.011	.080	2.6	.028
Dominican Republic	DOM	.19	.17	.017	.176	4.2	.022
Egypt	EGY	.19	.11	.030	.055	—	.025
Peru	PER	.19	.26	.003	.184	5.8	.022
Morocco	MAR	.18	.12	.029	.097	—	.026
Thailand	THA	.18	.08	.043	.185	5.1	.019
Paraguay	PRY	.17	.15	.019	.179	4.7	.031
Sri Lanka	LKA	.16	.14	.017	.129	5.4	.014
El Salvador	SLV	.15	.18	.007	.071	3.6	.013
Bolivia	BOL	.14	.13	.016	.072	4.3	.025
Jamaica	JAM	.14	.18	.006	.149	4.2	.010
Indonesia	IDN	.14	.07	.037	.255	3.8	.018
Bangladesh	BGD	.13	.11	.019	.033	2.0	.022
Philippines	PHL	.13	.12	.016	.163	6.5	.024
Pakistan	PAK	.13	.08	.027	.098	1.9	.031
Congo	COG	.12	.10	.020	.081	3.1	.033
Honduras	HND	.12	.13	.011	.121	3.6	.033
Nicaragua	NIC	.11	.21	−.007	.126	3.8	.027
India	IND	.09	.07	.020	.144	3.0	.021
Ivory Coast	CIV	.08	.08	.014	.084	—	.037
Papua New Guinea	PNG	.08	.09	.010	.150	1.6	.023

(*continued*)

TABLE B.2 (CONTINUED)

Country	Code	$\hat{y}_{90}$	$\hat{y}_{60}$	$g(60, 90)$	s_K	u	n
Guyana	GUY	.08	.23	−.021	.199	5.1	.005
Cape Verde Is.	CPV	.07	.06	.023	.264	—	.025
Cameroon	CMR	.07	.05	.021	.118	2.2	.028
Zimbabwe	ZWE	.07	.09	.002	.131	2.6	.034
Senegal	SEN	.07	.09	.003	.038	2.4	.029
China	CHN	.06	.04	.024	.222	—	.014
Nigeria	NGA	.06	.05	.016	.102	—	.030
Lesotho	LSO	.06	.02	.043	.176	3.5	.028
Zambia	ZMB	.06	.11	−.008	.098	4.3	.035
Benin	BEN	.05	.08	−.001	.089	0.7	.031
Ghana	GHA	.05	.08	−.003	.044	3.2	.033
Kenya	KEN	.05	.06	.009	.126	3.1	.037
Gambia	GMB	.05	.05	.013	.083	0.8	.032
Mauritania	MRT	.04	.09	−.009	.173	—	.024
Guinea	GIN	.04	.04	.018	.050	—	.025
Togo	TGO	.04	.03	.023	.146	2.1	.033
Madagascar	MDG	.04	.10	−.013	.015	—	.029
Mozambique	MOZ	.04	.08	−.006	.017	1.1	.026
Rwanda	RWA	.04	.04	.016	.058	0.8	.029
Guinea-Bissau	GNB	.04	.04	.016	.146	0.6	.019
Comoros	COM	.03	.04	.005	.164	—	.036
Central African Republic	CAF	.03	.05	.002	.049	1.3	.026
Malawi	MWI	.03	.03	.015	.080	2.6	.033
Chad	TCD	.03	.08	−.017	.014	—	.024
Uganda	UGA	.03	.05	−.002	.018	1.9	.024
Mali	MLI	.03	.06	−.010	.066	0.8	.025
Burundi	BDI	.03	.04	.000	.076	—	.029
Burkina Faso	BFA	.03	.03	.010	.094	—	.026

BIBLIOGRAPHY

ABRAMOVITZ, MOSES. 1986. "Catching Up, Forging Ahead and Falling Behind." *Journal of Economic History* 46 (June): 385–406.

AGHION, PHILIPPE, AND PETER HOWITT. 1992. "A Model of Growth through Creative Destruction." *Econometrica* 60 (March): 323–51.

ARROW, KENNETH J. 1962. "The Economic Implications of Learning by Doing." *Review of Economic Studies* 29 (June): 153–73.

BARRO, ROBERT J. 1991. "Economic Growth in a Cross Section of Countries." *Quarterly Journal of Economics* 106 (May): 407–43.

BARRO, ROBERT J., AND JONGWHA LEE. 1993. "International Comparisons of Educational Attainment." *Journal of Monetary Economics* 32 (December): 363–94.

BARRO, ROBERT J., AND XAVIER SALA-I-MARTIN. 1996. "Convergence across States and Regions." *Brookings Papers on Economic Activity* pp. 107–58.

———. 1992. "Convergence." *Journal of Political Economy* 100 (April): 223–51.

———. 1995. *Economic Growth*. New York: McGraw-Hill.

BASU, SUSANTO, AND DAVID N. WEIL. 1996. "Appropriate Technology and Growth." NBER Working Paper no. 5865. Cambridge, MA: National Bureau of Economic Research.

BAUMOL, WILLIAM J. 1986. "Productivity Growth, Convergence and Welfare: What the Long-Run Data Show." *American Economic Review* 76 (December): 1072–85.

———. 1990. "Entrepreneurship: Productive, Unproductive, and Destructive." *Journal of Political Economy* 98 (October): 893–921.

BILS, MARK, AND PETER KLENOW. 1996. "Does Schooling Cause Growth or the Other Way Around?" GSB mimeo. Chicago: University of Chicago.

BLACK, FISCHER, AND MYRON S. SCHOLES. 1972. "The Valuation of Option Contracts and a Test of Market Efficiency." *Journal of Finance* 27 (May): 399–417.

COBB, CHARLES W., AND PAUL H. DOUGLAS. 1928. "A Theory of Production." *American Economic Review* 18 (March): 139–65.

COUNCIL OF ECONOMIC ADVISORS. 1997. *The Economic Report of the President.* Washington, D.C.: U.S. Government Printing Office.

DAVID, PAUL A. 1990. "The Dynamo and the Computer: An Historical Perspective on the Modern Productivity Paradox." *American Economic Association Papers and Proceedings* 80 (May): 355–61.

DE LONG, J. BRADFORD. 1988. "Productivity Growth, Convergence, and Welfare: Comment." *American Economic Review* 78 (December): 1138–54.

DE SOTO, HERNANDO. 1989. *The Other Path.* New York: Harper and Row.

DIAZ-ALEJANDRO, CARLOS. 1970. *Essays on the Economic History of the Argentine Republic.* New Haven, Conn.: Yale University Press.

DIXIT, AVINASH K., AND JOSEPH E. STIGLITZ. 1977. "Monopolistic Competition and Optimum Product Diversity." *American Economic Review* 67 (June): 297–308.

EASTERLY, WILLIAM, MICHAEL KREMER, LANT PRITCHETT, AND LAWRENCE SUMMERS. 1993. "Good Policy or Good Luck? Country Growth Performance and Temporary Shocks." *Journal of Monetary Economics* 32 (December): 459–83.

EASTERLY, WILLIAM, ROBERT KING, ROSS LEVINE, AND SERGIO REBELO. 1994. "Policy, Technology Adoption and Growth." NBER Working Paper no. 4681. Cambridge, MA: National Bureau of Economic Research.

ETHIER, WILFRED J. 1982. "National and International Returns to Scale in the Modern Theory of International Trade." *American Economic Review* 72 (June): 389–405.

FRIEDMAN, MILTON. 1992. "Do Old Fallacies Ever Die?" *Journal of Economic Literature* 30 (December): 2129–32.

GERSCHENKRON, ALEXANDER. 1952. "Economic Backwardness in Historical Perspective." In *The Progress of Underdeveloped Areas*, ed. Bert F. Hoselitz. Chicago: University of Chicago Press.

GREENWOOD, JEREMY, AND MEHMET YORUKOGLU. 1997. "1974." *Carnegie Rochester Conference Series on Public Policy* 46. Amsterdam: North-Holland.

GRILICHES, ZVI. 1991. "The Search for R&D Spillovers." *Scandinavian Journal of Economics* 94: 29–47.

GROSSMAN, GENE M., AND ELHANAN HELPMAN. 1991. *Innovation and Growth in the Global Economy*. Cambridge, MA: MIT Press.

HALL, ROBERT E., AND CHARLES I. JONES. 1996. "The Productivity of Nations." NBER Working Paper no. 5812. Cambridge, MA: National Bureau of Economic Research.

HARDIN, GARRETT. 1968. "The Tragedy of the Commons." *Science* 162 (December 13): 1243–48.

HEISENBERG, WERNER. 1971. *Physics and Beyond; Encounters and Conversations*. Trans. Arnold J. Pomerans. New York: Harper & Row.

HOBSBAWM, ERIC J. 1969. *Industry and Empire, from 1750 to the Present Day*. Vol. 3 of *Pelican Economic History of Britain*. Harmondsworth: Penguin.

JONES, CHARLES I. 1995a. "R&D-Based Models of Economic Growth." *Journal of Political Economy* 103 (August): 759–84.

———. 1995b. "Time Series Tests of Endogenous Growth Models." *Quarterly Journal of Economics* 110 (May): 495–525.

———. 1996. "Convergence Revisited." Stanford University mimeo.

———. 1997a. "On the Evolution of the World Income Distribution." *Journal of Economic Perspectives* 11.

———. 1997b. "The Upcoming Slowdown in U.S. Economic Growth." Stanford University mimeo.

KALDOR, NICHOLAS. 1961. "Capital Accumulation and Economic Growth." In *The Theory of Capital*, ed. F.A. Lutz and D.C. Hague. New York: St. Martins.

KNACK, STEPHEN, AND PHILIP KEEFER. 1995. "Institutions and Economic Performance: Cross-Country Tests Using Alternative Institutional Measures." *Economics and Politics* 7 (November): 207–27.

KREMER, MICHAEL. 1993. "Population Growth and Technological Change: One Million B.C. to 1990." *Quarterly Journal of Economics* 108 (August): 681–716.

———. 1996. "A Mechanism for Encouraging Innovation." M.I.T. working paper.

LANDES, DAVID S. 1990. "Why Are We So Rich and They So Poor?" *American Economic Association Papers and Proceedings* 80 (May): 1–13.

LUCAS, ROBERT E., JR. 1988. "On the Mechanics of Economic Development." *Journal of Monetary Economics* 22 (July): 3–42.

MADDISON, ANGUS. 1995. *Monitoring the World Economy 1820–1992*. Paris: Organization for Economic Cooperation and Development.

MANKIW, N. GREGORY, DAVID ROMER, AND DAVID WEIL. 1992. "A Contribution to the Empirics of Economic Growth." *Quarterly Journal of Economics* 107 (May): 407–38.

MOKYR, JOEL. 1990. *The Lever of Riches.* New York: Oxford University Press.

MULLIGAN, CASEY B., AND XAVIER SALA-I-MARTIN. 1993. "Transitional Dynamics in Two-Sector Models of Endogenous Growth." *Quarterly Journal of Economics* 108 (August): 739–74.

NELSON, RICHARD R., AND EDMUND S. PHELPS. 1966. "Investment in Humans, Technological Diffusion, and Economic Growth." *American Economic Association Papers and Proceedings* 56 (May): 69–75.

NORDHAUS, WILLIAM D. 1969. "An Economic Theory of Technological Change." *American Economic Association Papers and Proceedings* 59 (May): 18–28.

——— . 1994. "Do Real Output and Real Wage Measures Capture Reality? The History of Lighting Suggests Not." Cowles Foundation Discussion Paper no. 1078. New Haven, CT: Yale University.

NORTH, DOUGLASS C. 1981. *Structure and Change in Economic History.* New York: Norton.

NORTH, DOUGLASS C., AND ROBERT P. THOMAS. 1973. *The Rise of the Western World.* Cambridge, U.K.: Cambridge University Press.

PHELPS, EDMUND S. 1966. "Models of Technical Progress and the Golden Rule of Research." *Review of Economic Studies* 33 (April): 133–45.

PRITCHETT, LANT. 1997. "Divergence: Big Time." *Journal of Economic Perspectives* 11.

QUAH, DANNY. 1993. "Galton's Fallacy and Tests of the Convergence Hypothesis." *Scandinavian Journal of Economics* 95 (December): 427–43.

——— . 1996. "Twin Peaks: Growth and Convergence in Models of Distribution Dynamics." *Economic Journal* 106 (July): 1045–55.

REBELO, SERGIO. 1991. "Long-Run Policy Analysis and Long-Run Growth." *Journal of Political Economy* 96 (June): 500–521.

ROMER, PAUL M. 1986. "Increasing Returns and Long-Run Growth." *Journal of Political Economy* 94 (October): 1002–37.

——— . 1987. "Crazy Explanations for the Productivity Slowdown." In *NBER Macroeconomics Annual 1987*, ed. Stanley Fischer. Cambridge, MA: MIT Press.

——— . 1989. "Capital Accumulation in the Theory of Long Run Growth." In *Modern Business Cycle Theory*, ed. Robert J. Barro. Cambridge, MA: Harvard University Press.

_____ . 1990. "Endogenous Technological Change." *Journal of Political Economy* 98 (October): S71–S102.

_____ . 1993. "Two Strategies for Economic Development: Using Ideas and Producing Ideas." In *Proceedings of the World Bank Annual Conference on Development Economics, 1992*. Washington, D.C.: World Bank.

_____ . 1994. "The Origins of Endogenous Growth." *Journal of Economic Perspectives* 8 (Winter): 3–22.

ROSENBERG, NATHAN. 1994. *Exploring the Black Box: Technology, Economics, and History*. New York: Cambridge University Press.

SACHS, JEFFREY D., AND ANDREW WARNER. 1995. "Economic Reform and the Process of Global Integration." *Brookings Papers on Economic Activity* 1: 1–95.

SALA-I-MARTIN, XAVIER. 1990. "Lecture Notes on Economic Growth." NBER Working Paper no. 3563. Cambridge, MA: National Bureau of Economic Research.

SHELL, KARL. 1967. "A Model of Inventive Activity and Capital Accumulation." In *Essays on the Theory of Economic Growth*, ed. Karl Shell. Cambridge, MA: MIT Press.

SHLEIFER, ANDREI, AND ROBERT W. VISHNY. 1993. "Corruption." *Quarterly Journal of Economics* 108 (August): 599–618.

SIMON, JULIAN L. 1981. *The Ultimate Resource*. Princeton, NJ: Princeton University Press.

SMITH, ADAM. 1776 (1981). *An Inquiry into the Nature and Causes of the Wealth of Nations*. Indianapolis: Liberty Press.

SOBEL, DAVA. 1995. *Longitude: The True Story of a Lone Genius Who Solved the Greatest Scientific Problem of His Time*. New York: Walker.

SOLOW, ROBERT M. 1956. "A Contribution to the Theory of Economic Growth." *Quarterly Journal of Economics* 70 (February): 65–94.

_____ . 1957. "Technical Change and the Aggregate Production Function." *Review of Economics and Statistics* 39 (August): 312–20.

SPENCE, MICHAEL. 1976. "Product Selection, Fixed Costs, and Monopolistic Competition." *Review of Economic Studies* 43 (June): 217–35.

SUMMERS, ROBERT, AND ALAN HESTON. 1991. "The Penn World Table (Mark 5): An Expanded Set of International Comparisons, 1950–1988." *Quarterly Journal of Economics* 106 (May): 327–68.

UZAWA, HIROFUMI. 1965. "Optimum Technical Change in an Aggregative Model of Economic Growth." *International Economic Review* 6 (January): 18–31.

YOUNG, ALWYN. 1995. "The Tyranny of Numbers: Confronting the Statistical Realities of the East Asian Growth Experience." *Quarterly Journal of Economics* 110 (August): 641–80.

INDEX